Francine Williams   June 2011
2216 Sandy Creek Rd.
Commerce, GA

P. 93
P. 94
P. 167
P. 178
P. 198
P. 202

P. 157/158
P. 138
P. 135 **

¡Sabor!

A Passion for Cuban Cuisine

✳ ¡Sabor! ✳

A Passion for Cuban Cuisine

Ana Quincoces Rodriguez

Foreword by Marilyn Milian,
Judge of *The People's Court*

RUNNING PRESS
PHILADELPHIA · LONDON

Library of Congress Control Number: 2007942757

› ISBN 978-0-7624-3347-6

Cover and interior design by Amanda Richmond
Edited by Diana C. von Glahn
Photography by Steve Legato
Photography assistant: Nick Demou
Food styling on pages 16, 22, 27, 31, 34, 38, 46, 54, 60, 65, 72, 76, 92, 95, 96, 115, 118, 123, 126, 128, 139, 142, 147, 150, 159, 162, 165, 173, 174, 186, 199, 200, 205, 208, 215, 223, 224 by John Carpitella, assisted by James Harrell
Food styling on pages 86, 89, 109, 179, 181, 182, 192, 195 by Diana von Glahn
Prop styling by Amanda Richmond
Props provided by Crate & Barrel and Fosters Urban Homeware.
Typography: Requiem and Abadi MT.

The publishers would like to thank Foster's Urban Homeware for the use of their demonstration kitchen and some of the props used during the photo shoot. We would also like to thank Crate & Barrel for the generous use of their merchandise during the photo shoot. A very special thanks to Alberto Asen for his magic touch. . . .

Running Press Book Publishers
2300 Chestnut Street
Philadelphia, PA 19103-4371

Visit us on the web!
www.runningpresscooks.com

For Kati and Beba:
" . . . when you get the choice to sit it out or dance . . .
I hope you dance. "

And for Robert

CONTENTS

✳ ACKNOWLEDGMENTS ✳

LIKE A DELICIOUS RECIPE, A GREAT COOKBOOK is a masterful blend of quality ingredients. The best dishes are often a collaborative effort of more than one person. So many wonderful people have had a hand in this delectable stew. Perhaps that is why it is so very satiating.

I thank my family first and foremost for their unwavering support and almost giddy enthusiasm. Robert, thank you for embarking on this adventure with me, you are . . . everything. Kati and Beba, you are the driving force behind everything I do. Your pride in me fuels me. I am awed on a daily basis by the two of you. I am forever grateful and honored to be your mom. I wish I could celebrate this milestone with my Dad, my hero, who lost his courageous battle with Alzheimer's in 2007. His pride in me could never be contained. He would have enjoyed this so. I would especially like to thank my mom, from whom I learned just about everything you'll read in this book. I thank her for passing on that "nurturing" gene and for teaching me that a house where you eat out of takeout containers is not really a home. I thank my brother for always, albeit quietly, supporting my every endeavor and for willingly taste testing every recipe and loving every minute of it; and to my sister-in-law, Ana, who is convinced I am the best cook in the world. I thank my in-laws Lilia and Oscar for their support, but mostly I thank them for my husband who makes my world a more beautiful place to live. I thank my aunt and uncle Nene and Carmita for bragging about me to just about everyone who will listen. I hope you have not annoyed too many people. Of course, the support of an amazing group of friends is the backbone of any venture and I am very lucky in that regard. Silvia, thank you for your steadfast friendship and support. I will make a cook out of you yet! Glenda, you said I could do this and here I am. Thanks for believing in me more than I believed in myself. Thank you to Ivette and Lory for proving that true friendship does stand the test of time.

I must thank Amanda Richmond, the very talented designer of this book. Thank you for your patience and understanding, and for creating something I am so very proud of. Thank you too, Steve Legato, the amazing photographer I had the pleasure of working with on this book. Thank you for making what could have been an intimidating process two of the most fun days of my life. Finally, I'd like to thank Diana von Glahn, my wonderful editor. Thank you for believing in this project and for deciding that my voice is unique and meant to be heard. Despite the many hours dedicated to this book, it never once felt like work. Thank you all.

✳ FOREWORD ✳

WHETHER YOU ARE CUBAN, LOVE A CUBAN, OR JUST LOVE CUBAN food, you will love this book, packed with delicious recipes as well as tasty memories. Ana Quincoces Rodriguez manages to capture the youth and essence of the best moments of the Cuban exile experience . . . delicious food enveloped in warmth, love, and laughter.

Although books about Cuban cooking can be found in some bookstores, the bastardization of the food to convert it to nouvelle cuisine would make our grandmothers spin in their graves. It simply cannot be done; you cannot make Cuban food more elegant, less filling, or lighter. It is to be savored for its true value: comfort food of the tastiest order. If I have to live in a world where you cannot ever savor the *lechón* for the ambrosia that it is, I prefer to depart peacefully. I will simply take my portion, on Cuban bread, thank you. It cannot be improved upon, cannot be low carbed or lightened. It is refreshing to finally see a Cuban cook who not only realizes this, but embraces it with such gusto.

The Cuban exile experience has been both revered and reviled, politically and philosophically, for its passionate opinions throughout its history in the United States. The one thing we can all agree about is that our food is intoxicatingly delectable. What a pleasure this book will be for those who wish to remember a simpler time, when hours upon hours were spent enjoying each other's company as the cook in the family layered onions upon bell pepper upon garlic . . . forging real connections not electronic ones. Kudos to Ana for bringing all that tumbling back to us, and making us better cooks in the process.

Marilyn Milian
Judge of *The People's Court*

✴ PREFACE ✴

TECHNICALLY, THE SPANISH WORD "SABOR" MEANS FLAVOR. And because this is a cookbook, we are naturally using the word with regards to the flavor of Cuban cuisine. But we all know that flavor can encompass more than just food. There is the flavor of a place, of its people, of an entire culture. You can cook with *sabor*, speak with *sabor*, and of course dance with *sabor*! There is even a well-known ballad called "Sabor a Mi," which translates as "the flavor of me" or the "taste of me" . . . but we won't go there. *Sabor*, as far as I'm concerned, is a state of mind and a way of life. It connotes a lively independence, a delicious flair, and a relaxed elegance. Even the word rolls off the tongue beautifully (especially if you can roll your "r"s).

All cuisines have their own distinct flavor and feel, but I am partial to—you guessed it—Cuban cuisine. As far as I'm concerned, Cuban food is meant to be made and eaten, savored and enjoyed with family and friends. That is why this book is so much more than just a collection of Cuban recipes. It is a peek, a little window if you will, into the life, the flavor—or *sabor*—of all things Cuban. But don't worry, you don't have to be Cuban to enjoy this book. This book is for everyone who enjoys food. You can be half Cuban, a quarter Cuban, married to a Cuban, dating a Cuban, or have a Cuban best friend. You can feel a special affinity towards Cubans because you enjoy the food, the music, or the *salsa* (pun intended). Maybe you're simply in a Cuban mood or are planning a Cuban-themed party so you and your guests can eat Cuban food and dance to Cuban music.

Everything about our heritage seems to be back in vogue these days. Cuban cigars, the ever-popular classic drink, "mojito," and of course the music! Cuban music moves you, making even the painfully shy involuntarily move in their seats. You just can't help but tap your fingers on the table or your feet on the floor once the bongos have begun to play.

While Cuban culture is the epitome of *sabor*, there is no better example of that Cuban flavor than Cuban women. We tend to be a little more mysterious, a little more curvaceous—not fat! Curvaceous! We love to cook and—no surprise here—we love to eat. Contrary to popular waif wisdom, men love curves. Especially Cuban men. They appreciate a woman who can cook and eat! The notion that a woman is somehow more fabulous because she nibbles on celery sticks all day or because the only thing she can manage to make for dinner are reservations is . . . well, sad.

Cuban cuisine encourages us to nurture a seemingly lost art. Cooking and feeding our loved ones is a very satisfying, yet seldom embraced, concept. Cuban food, in particular, is substantial and abundant. It's spicy. It's delectable. And it's always brimming with *Sabor*!

Cuban women are nurturers, an art that seems to have been lost nowadays. Cooking for others can be incredibly satisfying, and the food we feed our loved ones shows that, It is substantial and abundant. It's spicy. It's delectable. And it's always brimming with *sabor*! When we eat the food of our land, we are never left feeling hungry, and are always completely satisfied. Which is why I wanted to write this book. I think we can all stand to feel this way from time to time, and when you make the recipes within these pages, you are certain to feel that way, too.

☀ WHAT MAKES THIS BOOK DIFFERENT ☀

NOW, IF YOU HAPPEN TO BE CUBAN, YOU MAY REMEMBER "the" two cookbooks that defined our cuisine. You probably even have one lying around somewhere. Your grandmother definitely had one, your mother had one, and even your neighbor had one. These books—*Cocina Criolla* and *Cocina al Minuto*—were considered a staple in every Cuban home. One had a lovely "barbicide" blue cover and yellowing pages that look to have been typed on a 1940s Smith Corona. The other was pink with a June Cleaver-like caricature gracing the cover. If you were fortunate, like me, your mother had the foresight to laminate her copy with a spiffy avocado green and yellow contact paper that has resisted years of splattering oil and dripping sauces. These books are great to have around for nostalgic purposes—I keep mine in a safe place and refer to them from time to time, but almost never cook from them—they were first published decades ago in Spanish (using metric measurements, mind you) and later translated. The end result is cookbooks that are dated and just not very user friendly.

Then there are the newer generation of Cuban cookbooks: the "we are reinventing the wheel" genre of cookbooks. Some call it *nouveau*—or is it *nouvelle?*—*cuisine*. Or I know, better yet: *fusion!* I still can't figure out what they're fusing. Oh yeah, I forgot M-A-N-G-O! Yup. That seems to be the mindset with regards to Cuban cuisine these days. In a nutshell, if you add mango sauce to anything . . . it's Cuban. I'll let you in on a little secret: *real Cuban food contains absolutely, positively, no mango of any kind.* No sauce, no purée, no chutney, no infusion, no reduction, and no *coulis.* I promise.

The idea behind this book is that there is no need to tamper with perfection. Cuban food cannot be duplicated or combined with anything to make it better. It is what it is—and what it is is damn good!

And don't worry, I won't bombard you with a ton of complicated recipes. While this book contains a comprehensive collection of Cuban favorites, this is by no means the whole picture. Cuban food is diverse and the recipes available are plentiful. But, not to toot my own horn—ok, who am I kidding? Toot! Toot!—these recipes are good; real good. You'll enjoy making them, serving them, and eating them. You'll get rave reviews, make people happy, and create harmony in the universe . . . Ok, so I get a little carried away sometimes. *Buen provecho!* Enjoy!

☀ SOME BASICS ☀

IF YOU WERE BORN AND RAISED IN A CUBAN HOUSEHOLD, you probably already know what I am about to tell you here. I will nevertheless state some things for the benefit of those of you who are experimenting with Cuban cuisine for the very first time.

The main thing you should know when cooking and indulging in Cuban food is that your house will smell like Cuban food, your clothes will smell like Cuban food, and your hair will smell like Cuban food. My friend Glenda refers to this phenomenon as "Eau de Cuban House." Depending on the ventilation in your home, this glorious aroma may last well into the following day. If you grew up in a Cuban household, you'll remember that the smell never really went away. But don't let this discourage you. It is by no means unpleasant. In fact, to most Cubans, it's as inviting as the aroma of fresh bread baking.

In order to make many of the dishes in this book, you need to be in possession of three essential items. Get in your car, or better yet, walk (you'll need to burn calories to eat this stuff) to your local market and arm yourself with a head of garlic, a green bell pepper, and a large Spanish onion. Look at them, smell them, massage them. Become familiar with them because they make up the holy trinity of Cuban cooking. These vegetables are the foundation of one of the essential ingredients in Cuban cuisine—*sofrito*. I've included the recipe on page 14. It is the base, the heart and soul, the flavor, the *salsa* (if you will) of almost everything we cook. Without it, we would cease to exist! A little dramatic, no? What can I say, I'm passionate about my *sofrito*.

With respect to olive oil, we don't generally use Italian extra-virgin olive oil that is subtle in flavor and light in color and aroma. We use the hard-core stuff—so pungent and dark, it's almost green. This kind of olive oil is usually packaged in a rectangular tin can with a Spanish dancer on it. Any good quality olive oil from Spain will do. It really adds so much depth to a dish. In this book, whenever I call for olive oil, I highly recommend you use Spanish olive oil, but in a pinch you can use any good quality olive oil.

I also suggest you use large Spanish onions in these recipes because they add agreat flavor. However, white or yellow onions work well too. There are a few ingredients in these recipes, like *chorizo* (Spanish sausage), that I would not recommend substituting with anything else. You are just going to have to go out and hunt for some of these ingredients! But don't worry, most of them are very easy to find. To make things even easier, I've provided you with a glossary of traditional Cuban ingredients in the back of the book. And I've also recommended a few online stores to make your shopping even easier.

Another Cuban staple is the bay leaf. If you grew up in a Cuban household, you spent many a night fishing out the bay leaf from that evening's creation. If you are anything like me, you must have been convinced that there was some kind of conspiracy, since the bay leaf always found its way onto your plate.

Lastly, there's Cuban bread. Cuban bread is similar to French bread except that it is made with lard instead of oil. It is baked a little differently, too, placed in a cold oven over boiling water before it reaches its desired baking temperature. It is a delicious part of Cuban cuisine and a must for Cuban sandwiches. Almost every Cuban household has at least one loaf of Cuban bread at the table at all times. Because it is so good, the loaf is usually hollowed out while it's still warm. No one ever admits to the disembowelment of the loaf. The culprit, however, is inevitably revealed when he or she refuses the standard second helping of that evening's fare. Most Cuban families buy Cuban bread instead of making it, so I've given you the names and websites of a few places that sell Cuban bread in the back of the book. In most instances, French bread is a suitable alternative. There is also a great backup to Cuban bread—Cuban crackers. Every Cuban household has Cuban crackers. They are as basic as running water. Although they are tasty on their own, Cuban crackers are almost always used as a vehicle for transporting your food to your fork.

Sofrito
BASIC TOMATO-BASED SAUCE

Sofrito *is the foundation of many Cuban dishes. It is also a wonderful condiment, especially with store-bought roast chicken and sautéed mushrooms. This* sofrito *can be stored in the refrigerator for up to 5 days in a tightly sealed container.*

¼ cup olive oil

1 large onion, chopped

4 garlic cloves, minced

1 medium green bell pepper, chopped

1 cup tomato sauce

1 bay leaf

¼ cup *vino seco*
  (dry white cooking wine)

1 teaspoon salt

½ teaspoon pepper

½ teaspoon dried
  oregano leaves

½ teaspoon ground cumin

Heat the olive oil in a large frying pan over medium heat. Add the onion, garlic, and bell pepper, and sauté until the onion is translucent, 5 to 7 minutes. Add the tomato sauce, bay leaf, and vino seco, and cook 5 minutes more. Reduce the heat to low, add the salt, pepper, oregano, and cumin, and stir. Cover the pan and let the vegetables simmer for 10 to 15 minutes. Remove and discard the bay leaf.

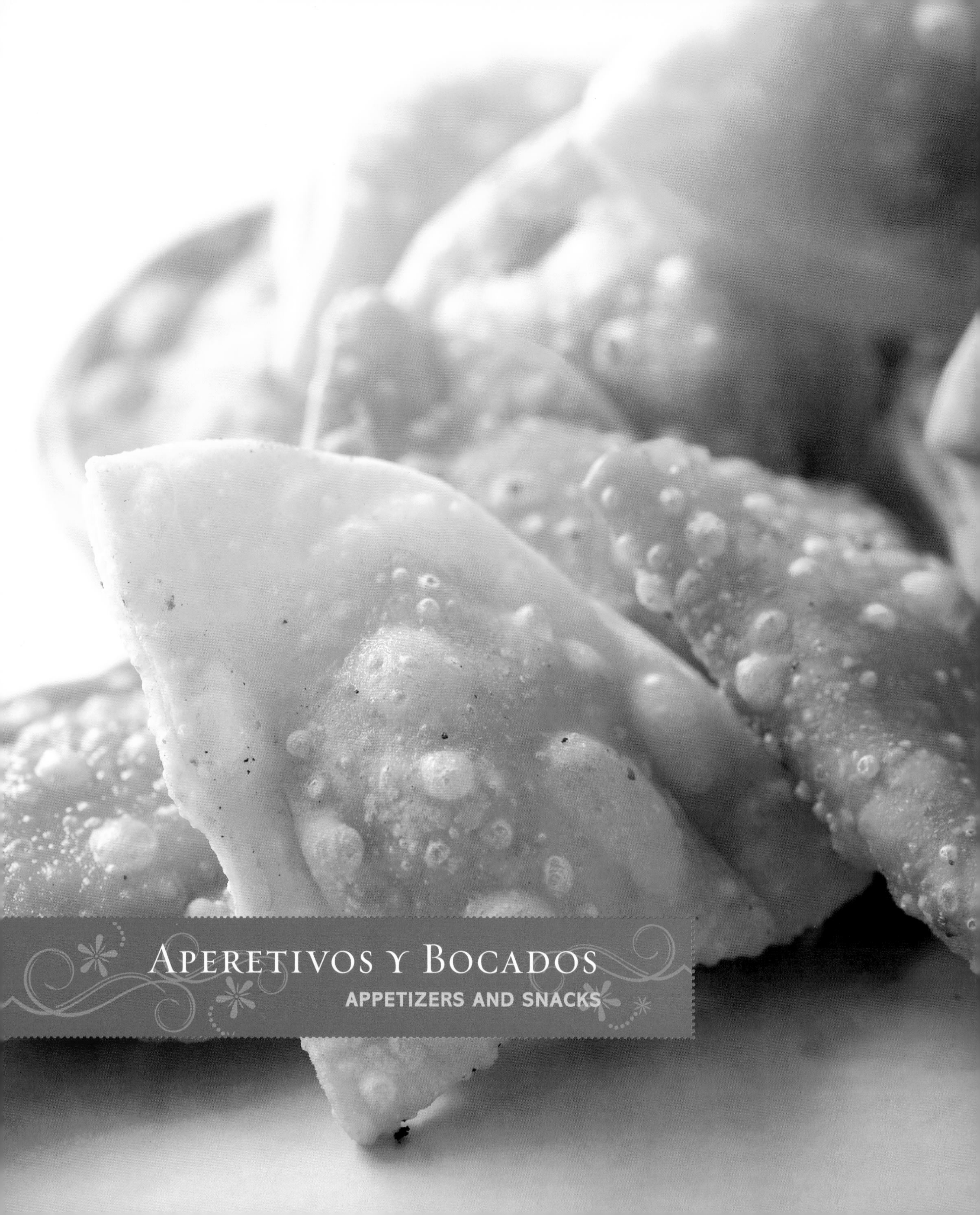

Aperetivos y Bocados

APPETIZERS AND SNACKS

For as long as I can remember, a large group of families, including my own, converge yearly on a small island called Sanibel on the Gulf Coast of Florida. We rent somewhat modest but comfortable two bedroom condos that face the ocean. There is nothing particularly grand about Sanibel. Frankly, the beaches aren't even that great, compared to Miami Beach. There is something about it, though. No matter how many luxury hotels I stay in or exotic locations I visit, there is something about being at Sanibel that I would not trade for the world. The second we cross the bridge onto the island, the decompression begins, during which the stresses of everyday life seem to disappear. The best pictures I have of my family have been taken in Sanibel. The large group of familiar faces, many of which we haven't seen since the previous year, is also very comforting. I think the beauty of this place is that it is the closest our parents can get to what life was like in Cuba: the island, food, family, friends, rum . . . food, (did I say that already?) are all reminiscent of their native land. Well, except for the small detail that it's not Cuba, and remember, everything was better in Cuba.

The patriarch of the family that began the annual pilgrimage to Sanibel, Reynaldo or *El Alcalde* (the mayor), as we affectionately call him, is largely responsible for keeping the tradition of visiting the island alive. Each morning, he prepares bottles and bottles of a deliciously addictive concoction of rum and juices that he calls "Whammy." He shares this recipe with no one, mind you. I suspect that his wife of more than 40 years is not even privy to the sacred formula. (Don't despair . . . I got my hands on it anyway. You can find it on page 222.) Around half an hour after drinking the first glass of the stuff (no one can drink just one), the sexagenarians* begin to find humor in the most mundane and ordinary things. The women begin to giggle like school girls and—I kid you not—flirt, yes, *flirt*, with the purveyor of this delicious libation.

* The word sexagenarian refers to those between 60 and 69 years of age. It is no coincidence that the word "sex" is involved. After all, Cubans are sex-y, even at 60!

Then there's the tent. Each and every morning around 10 a.m., the tent (*la carpa*) goes up. It happens as if by magic. Mind you, this is no small tent. It is at least 15 feet in each direction and requires large stakes and the effort of four men to put it up and take it down. But nobody really seems to mind; there are always plenty of volunteers willing to aid in the task. Especially when the afternoon storms come in—and they *always* come in. There is also a small sailboat called "Tin Tin," as well as a couple of kayaks. Once the storm "looks like" it's coming, the meteorologists in the group (all Cuban men over the age of 40 are self-proclaimed meteorologists) begin to predict its course and time of landfall. Of course, they are never right. Once the storm is upon us and the wind seems like it's blowing 100 miles an hour, the mad rush begins. Beach umbrellas and chairs become airborne, "Tin Tin" becomes in danger of capsizing, the kids in the kayaks are crying, and *El Alcalde* needs help with the tent. Heavy sigh. Somehow it all gets done and tomorrow the whole process begins again.

Not to be overlooked, however, is how we manage to stay sober enough—after all those "Whammies"—to be useful in a time of crisis. The answer is easy: it's the food that accompanies the beverages. The food on this vacation is as varied and unique as the loving hands that prepare it. By "food," I refer to the appetizer-type munchies that make their way to the tent on a consistent basis throughout the day. Everyone makes something different, and everyone has a favorite. My specialty are *Empanadas de Chorizo* (Chorizo Sausage Turnovers) but my favorite, by far, is my friend Guillermo's *Queso Brie Envuelto con Guayaba* (Brie and Guava en Croûte).

Once the food begins to arrive, those in the ocean doing the "Cuban Squat"* begin their mass exodus to land. Some, in a preemptive attempt to secure dibs on a particular food, will yell from a distance, *"¡Oye! ¡Guardame una!"* (Hey! Save me one!) or *"¡No seas tan gandido!"* (Don't be such a glutton!). Basically, it's survival of the fittest in our little beach jungle, but it's a delicious and enjoyable struggle. I'm sure that once you taste the treats in this chapter, you will understand why.

* A phenomenon by which a large group of Cubans congregates in such shallow water that, in order to submerse themselves to the shoulder, they must squat. It is not uncommon to see these squatters bobbing in the water for hours at a time, most of them with a "Whammy" in hand.

Pastica de Jamón
HAM SPREAD

When I was growing up, the little guy on the can of deviled ham always scared me. I mean, it's the devil!!! Pitchfork, tail, horns—the works! I'm not scared now, obviously, but when I was four, I was concerned that the devil—sometimes 3 or 4 devils (depending on how many cans my mom purchased at the store)—lived in my cupboard!! I could just imagine multiple devils talking to each other at night in the dark spaces of my home, conspiring on how to wipe out my entire family with their tiny little pitchforks! I know, I know, I may have been a good candidate for Prozac. . . .

That aside, this ham spread is versatile and delicious and a cinch to make. I always keep the ingredients on hand—just not in the cupboard.

SERVES 6 TO 8

- 2 (4.5-ounce) cans deviled ham
- 8 ounces cream cheese, at room temperature
- ½ teaspoon onion powder
- 1 teaspoon Worcestershire sauce
- Saltine crackers or soft rolls, for serving

Skim the fat off the top of the cans of the deviled ham and discard. Combine all of the ingredients in a small bowl and mix well with a fork to form a smooth paste. Cover with plastic wrap and refrigerate for at least 20 to 30 minutes.

Serve with saltine crackers or soft rolls.

Pastica de Pollo

CHICKEN SPREAD OR DIP

I like to call sandwiches made with these little spreads "hip" sandwiches. Not because they are hip, as in "cool," but because eating them will cause your hips to expand ever so slightly. The culprit is the creamy consistency of pastica. When paired with soft dinner rolls, they are simply irresistible. They make great little party sandwiches, especially when served with Croquetas *(pages 26–28) and* Papas Rellenas *(Stuffed Mashed Potato Balls) (page 35).*

SERVES 6 TO 8

½ cup mayonnaise

8 ounces cream cheese, at room temperature

1 tablespoon ketchup

½ teaspoon onion powder

1 teaspoon salt

½ teaspoon white pepper

1 teaspoon Worcestershire sauce

1 teaspoon hot sauce, optional

2 large boneless chicken breasts, poached or roasted, diced

Combine the mayonnaise, cream cheese, ketchup, onion powder, salt, pepper, Worcestershire sauce, and hot sauce in a large bowl and mix until very smooth. Add the chicken and mix to combine well. Taste and adjust the seasonings, if necessary. Serve with saltine crackers or spread on soft rolls as a snack.

Queso Brie Envuelto con Guayaba
BRIE AND GUAVA EN CROÛTE

I know what you are thinking: "Didn't Ana say that there would be nothing but authentic Cuban food in this book? Doesn't this en croûte *thing qualify as fusion?" Well, the answer is yes and yes. I know what I said. However, every rule has an exception and this is the exception. After all, I promised my friend Guillermo that, in return for betraying his father-in-law by divulging the secret recipe for the Whammy (see page 222), I would include his simple but scrumptious Brie and guava creation. I always keep my promises, especially when betrayal is involved. After you try this, you'll be glad that I did.*

SERVES 6 TO 8

1 (8-ounce) can Pillsbury crescent rolls

1 (8- to 10-ounce) round Brie cheese

½ cup guava preserves

1 egg, beaten

Crackers, for serving

Preheat the oven to 350°F. Spray a baking sheet with nonstick cooking spray.

Use a rolling pin to roll out the crescent roll dough into one rectangular sheet (ignore the perforations). Cut a 1-inch strip off each of the longer ends of the rectangle.

Carefully place the Brie in the center of the dough and pour the preserves on top. Fold the shorter edges of the dough over the Brie, then the two longer edges, and press to seal. Use the two strips of dough to make an X on top of the round, or roll each piece of dough into a little rosette and place them in the center of the Brie. (Obviously this is an optional step, but wouldn't Martha Stewart be proud if you did it?) Brush the top of the pastry with egg.

Bake the Brie for 15 to 20 minutes, until the dough is golden and flaky. Remove it from the oven and let it rest for 10 minutes before cutting into it. Serve with crackers.

Empanadas de Chorizo
CHORIZO TURNOVERS

Many Cuban bakeries in Miami bake empanadas, *which are small pastries that encase sweet or savory fillings. While the commercially made* empanadas *are delicious, they don't compare to these homemade treats. First of all, these* empanadas *are—you guessed it—fried. Second, this filling is a combination of chorizo and sweet ham, providing a delicate flavor balance. I've also given you two other options for making them—one with ground beef and the other with guava and cream cheese, for a sweet treat.*

I serve these chorizo empanadas *with a creamy* picante *dipping sauce that complements them perfectly. I invented this recipe many years ago, in an effort to find a nice appetizer to serve with mojitos and beer. I have been famous for them ever since. In fact, I cannot seem to fry them fast enough, and inevitably people burn their tongues trying to eat the* empanadas *before they have had a chance to cool.*

You can prepare the filling for empanadas *well in advance and freeze or refrigerate it until you're ready to proceed with the recipe. This recipe calls for frozen turnover pastry disks* (discos para empanadas)*, which are available at most major grocery stores in the Hispanic frozen food section (Goya makes some).*

MAKES 20 MEDIUM
or 40 APPETIZER-SIZED

Empanadas

2 tablespoons olive oil

1 garlic clove, minced

¼ cup diced onion

¼ cup diced green bell pepper

½ cup tomato sauce

¼ cup *vino seco*
  (dry white cooking wine)

¼ teaspoon pepper

¾ pound ground Spanish
  chorizo sausage

½ pound ground sweet ham

Salt

continued

To make the *empanadas*, heat the oil in a shallow pot over medium-high heat. Add the garlic, onion, and bell pepper, and sauté for 5 to 7 minutes, until soft. Add the tomato sauce, *vino seco*, and pepper, and cook for 5 to 7 minutes, stirring frequently. Add the chorizo and ham and continue cooking for an additional 5 minutes, stirring frequently. Turn the heat off and allow the mixture to cool to room temperature. Taste and add salt, if necessary.

Remove one package of the pastry disks from the refrigerator. (Always leave the ones you aren't working with in the refrigerator. They are easier to work with if they are firm.) Working on a lightly floured surface, separate the disks. If you are making appetizer-sized *empanadas*, cut each disk in half, creating two semicircles. If you are making the larger *empanadas*, leave the disks whole.

Place 1 to 1½ teaspoons of filling in the center of each half disk or 1 to 1½ tablespoons in the center of each whole disk. Fold each

continued

20 *discos para empanadas* (frozen turnover pastry disks), thawed and kept in the refrigerator

Canola oil, for shallow frying

Sauce

1 cup thick, refrigerated ranch dressing (I like Marie's)

1 to 2 tablespoons hot sauce (like Tabasco)

1 to 2 teaspoons chopped cilantro

half disk to make a small triangle or each whole disk to make a semicircle. Using the tines of a fork, press around the edges to seal.

If you do not plan to fry the *empanadas* immediately, cover them with a damp towel or place them in an airtight container and refrigerate them for up to 5 days.

Heat the oil in a deep pan to 350°F over medium heat. If you do not own an oil thermometer, dip the corner of one of the *empanadas* in the oil to check if it is hot enough. The oil should bubble around the dough.

Add the *empanadas*, about 4 to 5 at a time, to the oil and fry them for 3 to 4 minutes, turning them once, until they are golden brown. Transfer to a paper towel–lined plate and continue frying the rest of the *empanadas*.

To make the dipping sauce, combine the ranch dressing and hot sauce in a bowl and garnish with the cilantro. Serve in a small bowl alongside the hot *empanadas*.

Empanadas de Carne (Ground Beef Empanadas): Fill your *empanadas* with *picadillo* (page 144), omitting the potatoes. You can also use leftover *picadillo* for this.

Empanadas de Guayaba y Queso (Guava and Cream Cheese Empanadas): Fill the *empanadas* with 1-inch cubes of both guava paste and cream cheese. Make sure you use the full-fat cream cheese that comes in a bar.

Fina's Famous Carne Fría
MEAT ROLLS

Carne fría *literally means "cold meat." Now, I know that might not sound too appealing, but I assure you, this recipe is spectacular. You might also think that this recipe looks like a lot of work. I'm not going to lie and say it isn't time consuming, but I, and many Cubans, think it's worth the effort.* Carne fría *is delicious—no doubt about it. For many Cubans, this treat holds a certain level of nostalgia. But, if you didn't grow up eating* carne fría, *let me just say that when you do decide to take the plunge into the world of* carne fría, *Fina's recipe is the absolute best place to begin.*

SERVES 25 TO 30 AS AN APPETIZER

1 pound ground beef

1 pound ground pork

½ pound ground ham

1 small onion, diced

2 garlic cloves, minced

2 teaspoons salt

1 teaspoon prepared mustard

1 teaspoon Worcestershire sauce

⅛ teaspoon white pepper

⅛ teaspoon ground nutmeg

1⅛ teaspoon ground cumin

1⅛ teaspoon ground oregano

10 large eggs

2 cups cracker meal

1 large onion, halved

2 garlic cloves

1 bay leaf

1 teaspoon black peppercorns

Saltine crackers, for serving

Combine the ground beef, pork, and ham with the diced onion, minced garlic, 1 teaspoon of the salt, mustard, Worcestershire sauce, pepper, nutmeg, ⅛ teaspoon of the cumin, ⅛ teaspoon of the oregano, 4 eggs, and 1 cup of the cracker meal in a large bowl and knead until well mixed.

Place the remaining 6 eggs and the 1 cup cracker meal in two separate shallow baking dishes. Beat the eggs.

Divide the meat mixture into three parts, and shape them into 8-inch long by 3-inch wide cylindrical rolls. Roll each cylinder in the eggs and then the cracker meal. Wrap each roll with dampened cheesecloth and set aside.

Bring 2 quarts of water to a boil in a large pot. Add the halved onion, the whole garlic cloves, bay leaf, peppercorns, and remaining teaspoons of the salt, cumin, and oregano. Carefully place the cylinders of meat in the water, reduce the heat to medium, and cover the pot. Cook for 2 hours.

Remove the meat cylinders from the pot and remove the cheesecloth immediately. Allow the meat to cool well before slicing. Serve with saltines.

Croquetas de Jamón, Pollo, o Carne
HAM, CHICKEN, OR BEEF CROQUETTES

I love croquetas! I mean, what's not to love? These little fried bundles of creamy, meat-filled goodness are a favorite of young and old alike, and a quintessential part of any Cuban celebration. They are good in sandwiches, on crackers, or on their own; perfect for breakfast, lunch, or dinner. And they can be made with most any kind of meat, fish, or poultry—I've given you directions for making them with ham, chicken, or beef.

Although croquetas are perfectly acceptable at room temperature, they are best right out of the fryer—crispy on the outside, creamy and divine on the inside. These little treats are so flexible, they can be made in large quantities and frozen until ready to fry. So there's no reason why you should have to save these for parties or special occasions. In fact, I think they should add a fifth food group, exclusively for croquetas!

When I was a little girl, a neighborhood lady sold frozen and ready-to-fry croquetas door-to-door. She made them in two sizes—regular and party size. Because these are somewhat labor intensive, mine are somewhere in the middle—not too big, not too small. Feel free to make them whatever size you prefer. Serve them with saltine crackers and a squeeze of lime or in a croqueta preparada (page 64).

SERVES 6 TO 8

1½ to 2 pounds sweet ham, cooked chicken, or flank steak

2 cups whole milk

¼ pound (1 stick) salted butter

½ cup all-purpose flour

½ teaspoon salt, plus more as needed

½ teaspoon ground nutmeg

½ teaspoon white pepper, plus more as needed

2 tablespoons chopped parsley

2 cups ground cracker meal or bread crumbs

4 eggs

2 to 3 cups corn oil

To make ham or chicken croquettes: Grind the ham or chicken in a food processor until it is finely ground. Pour the ground meat—you should have about 3 cups—into a large mixing bowl, and set aside. To make beef croquettes: Place the steak in a large pot and add water to cover. Boil the steak for 2 hours, until it is tender. Drain the steak and let it cool. Grind the beef in a food processor until it is finely ground. Pour the ground meat—you should have about 3 cups—into a large mixing bowl, and set aside.

Bring the milk to a boil in a heavy saucepan.

Meanwhile, melt the butter over medium heat in a large saucepan, until it begins to bubble. Whisk in the flour, salt, nutmeg, and pepper. Reduce the heat to low and continue stirring until the flour mixture attains a light golden color. While whisking, add the hot milk ½ cup at a time, completely incorporating each addition before adding the next. Raise the heat to medium and bring the mixture to a boil. Continue stirring to avoid lumps. Once the béchamel has thickened, add it, little by little, to the ham, chicken, or beef and mix

continued

until the mixture has the consistency of soft Play-Doh. Add the parsley and combine well. Taste the mixture and add more salt and pepper, if necessary. This is particularly important with the beef and chicken croquettes. Set aside and allow the mixture to cool to room temperature, then refrigerate for at least 4 hours. This can be done a day or two ahead. Just be certain to keep the mixture in a tightly sealed container in the refrigerator so it doesn't dry up.

Place the cracker meal and the eggs in two separate bowls. Shape a heaping tablespoon of the meat mixture into a cylinder about 1 inch in diameter and 2½ inches long. Dip the cylinder in the egg, then in the cracker meal, then again in the egg, and again in the cracker meal. Place the *croqueta* on a baking sheet and repeat with the remaining meat mixture. Refrigerate for at least 6 hours. (This can be done a day or days in advance.) The longer you refrigerate them, the better your end result. I always refrigerate mine overnight.

Heat about 3 inches of oil in a large frying pan to 375°F over medium-high heat. Add 5 to 6 *croquetas* to the hot oil and fry them for 2 to 3 minutes, until golden brown on all sides. Do not fry too many of the *croquetas* at once and be sure to let the oil come back to 375°F before adding the next batch. Drain the fried *croquetas* on paper towels.

Frituras—Quatro Variaciones
FRITTERS—FOUR VARIATIONS

Cubans are big on fritters, basically because we're big on frying, which has been well established. Here, I've given you four variations on the fritter theme—cod, corn, crab, and malanga. They are all super easy to make and undeniably delicious. Give me a cold beer and these delicious fritters, and I am one happy Cuban. I know, I'm easy. . . . To please, that is. The problem is trying to eat just one. So fry these up quickly, because they go fast!

FRITURAS DE BACALAO
Cod Fritters

SERVES 6 TO 8

1 pound salt cod

4 large eggs, beaten

6 tablespoons all-purpose flour

1 teaspoon baking powder

3 tablespoons grated white onion

2 tablespoons diced parsley

¼ teaspoon white pepper

½ teaspoon paprika

2 to 3 cups corn oil

Hot sauce, for serving

Lime wedges, for serving

Place the cod in a large bowl and add enough water to cover. Soak the cod at room temperature for 10 to 12 hours, changing the water frequently.

Place the cod in a large pot and add enough water to cover. Bring to a boil and boil for 1 hour over medium-high heat, adding more water as necessary. Transfer the cod to a plate and set aside to cool.

Pick out any bones from the cod, then chop it finely. Set aside.

Combine the eggs, flour, baking powder, onion, parsley, pepper, and paprika in a large bowl and mix well. Add the cod and mix until it is fully incorporated into the batter.

In a large heavy pot, heat 2 to 3 inches of oil to about 375°F over medium-high heat.

Drop the batter by heaping tablespoons into the hot oil; the fritters should puff up a little. Fry for about 4 minutes, turning the fritters when the edges look golden, after about 2 minutes. Transfer the fritters to a paper towel–lined plate and serve immediately with hot sauce and lime wedges.

SERVES 6 TO 8

2 cups canned or frozen
   corn kernels, thawed
   (not creamed corn)
1 garlic clove, minced
3 tablespoons minced
   sweet onion
3 large eggs, beaten
3 tablespoons whole milk
1 tablespoon sugar
1 teaspoon salt
1 teaspoon baking powder
½ teaspoon white pepper
½ teaspoon paprika
5 tablespoons all-purpose flour
2 to 3 cups canola oil

Combine the corn, garlic, onion, eggs, milk, sugar, salt, baking powder, pepper, paprika, and 4 tablespoons of flour in a food processor or blender and blend well. Add the additional tablespoon of flour if the batter does not hold together on a tablespoon (it should be thick).

Heat about 2 inches of oil in a large frying pan over medium-high heat. Drop the batter by heaping tablespoons into the hot oil; the fritters should puff up a little. Fry for about 4 minutes, turning the fritters when the edges look golden, after about 2 minutes. Transfer the fritters to a paper towel–lined plate and serve immediately with cold beers all around.

FRITURAS DE CANGREJO
Crab Fritters

3 tablespoons whole milk

3 large eggs

1 garlic clove, minced

3 tablespoons minced sweet
   onion

1 teaspoon baking powder

1 teaspoon salt

½ teaspoon white pepper

½ teaspoon paprika

¾ cup all-purpose flour

½ pound cooked crab, picked
   clean of bones and cartilage

2 tablespoons fresh parsley,
   chopped

2 to 3 cups canola oil

Combine the milk, eggs, garlic, onion, baking powder, salt, pepper, paprika, and flour in a food processor or blender and blend well. The batter should be thick. Pour the mixture into a bowl and fold in the crab and parsley, fully incorporating all the ingredients.

Heat about 2 inches of oil in a large frying pan over medium-high heat. Drop the batter by heaping tablespoons into the hot oil; the fritters should puff up a little. Fry for about 4 minutes, turning the fritters when the edges look golden, after about 2 minutes. Transfer the fritters to a paper towel–lined plate and serve immediately.

Note: It is not essential that you use a food processor or a blender for this recipe. A bowl and wooden spoon work just as well, they just require a little more elbow grease. Just be sure to fold in the crab and parsley last.

FRITURAS DE MALANGA
Malanga Fritters

SERVES 6 TO 8

2 cups peeled and cubed
malanga, boiled for 3 minutes

2 large eggs

1 garlic clove, minced

3 tablespoons minced sweet
onion

1 teaspoon salt

½ teaspoon white pepper

½ teaspoon paprika

2 tablespoons all-purpose flour

2 to 3 cups canola oil

Combine the *malanga*, eggs, garlic, onion, salt, pepper, paprika, and flour in a food processor or blender and blend well. The batter should be thick.

Heat about 2 inches of oil in a large frying pan over medium-high heat. Drop the batter by heaping tablespoons into the hot oil; the fritters should puff up a little. Fry for about 4 minutes, turning the fritters when the edges look golden, after about 2 minutes. Transfer the fritters to a paper towel–lined plate and serve immediately.

Papas Rellenas
STUFFED MASHED POTATO BALLS

Papas Rellenas are uniquely Cuban, although they are basically portable meat and potatoes. These are a little labor intensive, but are well worth the effort. What makes them great is that they can be made in large batches, like the croquetas, *then frozen.* Papas rellenas *are great party treats that can also be made in assorted sizes. Of course, in my opinion, the best size is large . . . always large!*

SERVES 6 TO 8

Potatoes

3 pounds Yukon gold potatoes, peeled and cut into 2-inch pieces

2 garlic cloves

¼ cup whole milk, warm

4 tablespoons butter, melted

¼ cup heavy cream, warm

2 teaspoons salt

½ teaspoon white pepper

Picadillo

¼ cup olive oil

2 garlic cloves, minced

1 medium onion, diced

1 small green bell pepper, diced

1 pound ground sirloin or ground round

¼ cup *vino seco* (dry white cooking wine)

1 cup tomato sauce

2 tablespoons tomato paste

1 teaspoon salt

½ teaspoon pepper

continued

To make the mashed potatoes, bring 2 quarts of water to a boil in a large pot. Add the potatoes and garlic. Reduce the heat to medium and cook the potatoes, partially covered, for 25 to 30 minutes, until they are fork-tender.

Combine the milk, butter, and cream in a bowl.

Drain the potatoes into a colander, remove and discard the garlic cloves, and return the potatoes to the pot. Using a handheld mixer, beat the potatoes until they break apart. Add the milk mixture little by little while still beating. Don't beat too much—these should be more firm than typical mashed potatoes. Once all the ingredients are fully incorporated, add the salt and pepper. Taste and adjust the seasonings, if necessary. Set aside to cool.

To make the *picadillo*, heat half the olive oil in a large frying pan over medium-high heat. Add the garlic, onion, and bell pepper, and sauté until tender, for 5 to 7 minutes. Raise the heat to medium-high and add the ground beef—the meat should make a searing sound when it hits the pan; if it doesn't, increase the heat to high for a few minutes before adding the meat. Stir frequently to break up any large chunks of meat. Cook, stirring frequently, for 5 to 7 minutes, until the beef is thoroughly cooked (no longer red). Drain any excess liquid from the pan. Add the *vino seco*, tomato sauce, tomato paste, salt, pepper, cumin, oregano, and the remaining olive oil to the pan. Reduce the heat to low and simmer, uncovered, for about 20 minutes.

continued

½ teaspoon ground cumin

½ teaspoon ground oregano

¼ raisins, optional

¼ cup chopped
     pimento-stuffed olives

2 tablespoons capers

Assembly

Canola oil

4 large eggs, lightly beaten

2 cups cracker meal

Add the raisins, olives, and capers, and set aside to cool.

To assemble the *papas rellenas*, coat your hands lightly with olive or canola oil. Shape a spoonful of mashed potatoes into a 3-inch ball. Poke a hole in the center of the ball and fill it with about 2 tablespoons of *picadillo*; seal it completely. Repeat this step with all the mashed potatoes and *picadillo*, making certain that the balls are uniform in size.

Roll the potato balls in egg, then in cracker meal. Repeat this step with all the potato balls. Place them on a baking sheet and refrigerate for at least 4 hours.

Heat 3 inches of oil in a large frying pan over medium-high heat. Fry the potato balls for 5 to 7 minutes, turning them frequently until they are crispy and golden brown on all sides. Drain on a paper towel–lined platter. Serve immediately.

Soups are an integral part of Cuban cuisine. They are the foundation of every meal, providing heartiness and warmth, the two most important aspects of any Cuban meal. But don't think that these soups are the watery, overly salted soups that many of us are, unfortunately, used to. I mean, when you think of soup, don't you envision some type of broth-like substance? Well, these soups are nothing like that; they are thick and substantial. In fact, many of them include beans and, of course, savory *sofrito*, the heart of Cuban cuisine.

Almost every childhood meal I remember involved beans or legumes of some kind. I would often wake up to the wonderful aromas of soup—be it black bean, red bean, split pea, lentil, or a variety of others. It wasn't so much the aromas that woke me, but the soothing sound that only a pressure cooker can make. Many Cuban women begin cooking early in the day. It's a habit that began back in Cuba, when husbands came home from work at lunchtime for a little, you know, soup. Lunch would be announced by the *ding!* of the Hitachi (the rice cooker all Cubans use). Later that evening, a meat would be added to the meal, as well as some fried vegetables, a salad (though rarely), and a loaf of Cuban bread (which had inevitably been hollowed out during lunchtime).

Cuban sandwiches are also unlike their American counterparts. In fact, the word *sandwich* doesn't really do these recipes justice. While you might envision slapping two pieces of Wonder bread together with cheese or meat and maybe some unfortunate-looking pieces of lettuce, these sandwiches are a far cry from your typical "turkey on whole wheat, hold the mayo." These babies are hot and satisfying. Stay with me; I'm still talking sandwiches here.

Pretty much everyone has heard of the Cuban Sandwich or *Sanwich Cubano*, as it's referred to at most Cuban establishments. If you haven't, you must make one of these immediately. They are simply irresistible. *Pan con Bistec*, or Steak Sandwich, is also a popular item that is equally delectable. In addition to these fine recipes, I show you how to make other traditional Cuban favorites, like the *Frita* (Cuban-Style Hamburger), *Medianoche* (Midnight Sandwich), and *Croqueta Preparada* (Croquette Sandwich). So prepare yourself for a unique sandwich experience, a festival of flavors, and the kind of satisfaction you could never get from tuna on rye.

Frijoles Negros
BLACK BEAN SOUP

You will find a recipe for black bean soup in every Cuban cookbook. It's mandatory. I'm not kidding; I actually think there is some kind of publishing law that requires it. But don't be fooled—not all black beans are created equal. While I'd love to tell you that mine are the absolute best—well, they are—I suppose there may be some other marginally good recipes out there. What is certain is that black beans are considered the food of the gods by most Cubans. One taste of this recipe, and you'll see why.

Soaking your beans the night before you cook them makes the cooking process much quicker and produces beans that are uniformly tender.

SERVES 6 TO 8

1 pound dry black beans, picked through and rinsed

¼ cup olive oil

1 large onion, chopped

3 garlic cloves, minced

1 green bell pepper, chopped

2 tablespoons tomato paste

1 bay leaf

½ teaspoon ground cumin

½ teaspoon dried oregano leaves

2 tablespoons red wine vinegar

1 tablespoon sugar

½ cup *vino seco* (dry white cooking wine)

Salt and pepper

6 to 8 cups *Arroz Blanco* (White Rice) (page 82), for serving

Place the beans in a large bowl and add enough room temperature water to cover. Soak the beans for at least 6 hours, preferably overnight. (If you are soaking them for only 6 hours, use slightly warm or tepid water instead.)

Place a medium to large sieve over a large bowl and drain the beans into the sieve, catching the soaking water in the bowl underneath. Measure the soaking liquid and add more water, if necessary, to equal 6 cups

Heat the olive oil in a large stockpot over medium heat. Add the onion, garlic, and bell pepper and sauté for 5 to 7 minutes, until the vegetables soften. Add the tomato paste, bay leaf, cumin, and oregano and stir well. Add the beans and soaking liquid mixture and bring to a boil.

Let the soup boil for about 5 minutes, then reduce the heat to low. Add the vinegar, sugar, and *vino seco*, and stir well. Cover the pot and let the soup simmer for 3 to 3½ hours, until the beans are soft and tender and the stock has thickened. (The stock will thicken as the beans cool to room temperature.) Remove and discard the bay leaf. Season the soup generously with salt and a sprinkling of pepper. Serve over long-grain white rice.

Frijoles Colorados

RED BEAN SOUP

Another favorite in Cuban cuisine, red bean soup is quite different from the ever-popular black bean soup. Here, the tomato base and chorizo impart a tangy and unique flavor to the beans. The addition of vegetables makes this a perfect one-dish meal: hearty and delicious.

Make sure you don't confuse these small, oval, red beans with kidney beans. And remember: soaking the beans overnight helps them cook more quickly and evenly. This soup may be served alone or over fluffy white rice.

SERVES 6 TO 8

1 pound dry red beans

¼ cup olive oil

1 large onion, diced

3 garlic cloves, minced

1 medium green bell pepper, chopped

½ pound Spanish chorizo sausage

¼ pound ham hock, optional

1 bay leaf

1 cup tomato sauce

½ cup *vino seco* (dry white cooking wine)

1 cup peeled and diced red-skinned potatoes

1 cup chopped *calabaza*

Salt and pepper

Place the beans in a large bowl and add enough room temperature water to cover. Soak the beans for at least 6 hours, preferably overnight. (If you are soaking them for only 6 hours, use slightly warm or tepid water instead.)

Place a medium to large sieve over a large bowl and drain the beans into the sieve, catching the soaking water in the bowl underneath. Measure the soaking liquid and add more water, if necessary, to equal 6 cups.

Heat the olive oil in a large stockpot over medium heat. Add the onion, garlic, and bell pepper and sauté for 5 to 7 minutes, until the vegetables soften.

Add the chorizo (I remove the casing before adding it, but it is not necessary) and the ham hock, and cook for 5 to 7 minutes to render some of the fat from the meat. Reduce the heat to low and add the bay leaf and tomato sauce. Continue cooking over low heat for another 5 minutes.

Add 1½ quarts water, the *vino seco*, and the beans and their soaking water, and raise the heat to high. Bring the soup to a boil, stirring frequently. Let the soup boil for 10 minutes.

Reduce the heat to low, cover the pot, and cook the soup for 2 to 2½ hours, until it thickens slightly. Remove the bay leaf, chorizo, and ham hock. Cut the chorizo into ½-inch slices and return them to the pot. Discard the bay leaf and ham hock.

Add the potatoes and the *calabaza*, and bring the soup to a boil. Reduce the heat to low and cover. Continue cooking over low heat until the vegetables are fork-tender. Add salt and pepper to taste.

Sopa de Pollo
CUBAN-STYLE CHICKEN SOUP

The only time I recall having soup as a full meal was when I was sick. The second my mother thought I had destemplanza (a mysterious Cuban malady, wherein your body temperature is one degree higher than normal, greatly increasing the probability of imminent death from pneumonia), she would begin a pot of chicken soup (also known as Cuban penicillin). Cuban chicken soup is by far the best chicken soup you'll ever taste. It reminds me of that commercial that advertises "the soup that eats like a meal." You literally could eat it with a fork instead of a spoon. I'm going to share with you a little known fact about Cuban chicken soup: years ago, when Harvard conducted that famous study proving that the consumption of chicken soup shortens the duration and severity of the common cold, it was Cuban chicken soup that was found to be most effective. Really, it's true. . . . All right, I'm lying. But you will feel better once you've had a bowl, whether you have a cold or not.

SERVES 6 TO 8

4 chicken breast halves, bone in, skins removed

1 garlic clove

1 bay leaf

1 teaspoon salt, plus more as needed

1 tablespoon tomato paste

2 tablespoons olive oil

1 medium onion, diced

2 celery stalks, diced

1 carrot, diced

1 cup chopped *calabaza*

1 cup chopped *malanga* or potatoes

4 ounces *fideos* or angel hair pasta

Pepper

Lime wedge, for serving

Bring 2 quarts of water to a boil in a large pot. Add the chicken, garlic, bay leaf, and salt. Reduce the heat to low, cover the pot, and simmer for 1 hour, or until the chicken is cooked through and opaque. Transfer the chicken to a plate and set aside. Discard the garlic and bay leaf. Transfer the stock to another container and allow it to cool completely.

In a small cup, dissolve the tomato paste in ½ cup of the stock.

Heat the oil in the same pot used to make the stock. Add the onion, celery, and carrot, and sauté for about 5 minutes, until the onion is soft and translucent. Add the *calabaza*, *malanga*, the tomato paste mixture, and the stock. The stock should cover the vegetables by 3 to 4 inches. If the stock is too low, add more water.

Bring the soup to a boil, then reduce the heat to low, cover the pot, and let the soup simmer until the vegetables are soft and tender, about 40 minutes.

Remove the chicken from the bone and tear it into pieces. (I prefer this method to chopping it because the chicken retains more moisture and flavor.) Add the chicken and the *fideos* to the stock and stir to incorporate. Bring the soup to a boil again, then turn off the heat and season the soup with salt and pepper to taste. Stir well and add a squeeze of lime before serving.

Sopa de Platano
PLANTAIN SOUP

If you were stranded on a deserted island with nothing but plantains and, say, this book, you certainly would have no shortage of recipes. The relationship Cubans have with plantains reminds me of Bubba's relationship to shrimp in Forrest Gump. *The variety of recipes is endless. This creamy and delectable plantain soup is a great start and a definite delight.*

SERVES 6

¼ cup olive oil

1 medium onion, diced

2 garlic cloves, minced

½ cup diced carrot

¼ cup diced celery

6 cups low-sodium beef stock

3 green plantains, peeled
   and diced

1 bay leaf

1 teaspoon salt

½ teaspoon ground cumin

½ teaspoon ground coriander

½ teaspoon pepper

½ teaspoon paprika

3 tablespoons fresh lime juice

Mariquitas (Plantain Chips)
   (page 99), for garnish

Heat the olive oil in a large, heavy pot over medium heat. Add the onion and garlic, and sauté for 5 minutes, until they both soften slightly. Add the carrot and celery and cook for another 5 minutes, stirring frequently. Add the remaining ingredients, raise the heat to high, and bring the soup to a rapid boil. Boil for 3 minutes, stirring frequently.

Reduce the heat to low, cover the pot, and simmer for 35 to 40 minutes, until the plantains are tender. Remove the pot from the heat and allow the soup to cool a bit. Remove and discard the bay leaf.

Using an immersion blender or working in small batches with a standard blender or food processor, purée the soup until it is creamy. Taste the soup and adjust the seasonings, if necessary. Serve hot, garnished with *Mariquitas* (Plantain Chips).

Sopa de Ajo
GARLIC SOUP

This soup is a tribute to the love that Cubans have for the mighty little garlic bulb. The health benefits of garlic are reason enough to make this wonderfully unique soup, and when you experience its flavors and aromas, you'll be glad you did.

SERVES 4

Croutons

2 garlic cloves, minced

3 tablespoons olive oil

½ teaspoon salt

2½ cups fresh 1-inch bread cubes

Soup

2 tablespoons olive oil

6 garlic cloves, minced

4 cups chicken stock

½ teaspoon paprika

½ teaspoon cayenne pepper

1 teaspoon salt

4 eggs

Chopped fresh flat-leaf parsley, for garnish

To make the croutons, preheat the oven to 375°F.

Combine the garlic, olive oil, and salt in a large bowl. Add the bread pieces and toss until they are coated with the oil mixture. Spread the bread cubes in a single layer on a baking sheet. Bake for 5 to 7 minutes, turning them once halfway through the baking process. Check them frequently to make sure they do not burn (raw garlic burns quickly).

To make the soup, heat the oil in a large stockpot over medium-low heat. Add the garlic and cook for 2 to 3 minutes, stirring frequently so it softens but does not burn. Add the stock, paprika, cayenne, and salt (depending on the stock you use, you might not need the salt). Remove the pot from the heat and set it aside until you are ready to serve.

Preheat the oven to 350°F.

Place 4 heatproof bowls—onion soup crocks work well for this—on a baking sheet. Pour 2 to 3 tablespoons of the soup into each bowl. Crack an egg into a bowl and beat it, lightly. Pour the egg into a soup crock, and repeat with the remaining eggs and soup bowls. Fill the bowls about three-quarters full with soup, then top with croutons.

Carefully transfer the baking sheet with the bowls to the oven, and bake for 5 minutes.

To serve, garnish the soup with parsley.

Note: If you make the soup in advance and let it sit until it comes to room temperature or is cold, reheat it on the stove before placing it in the oven.

Sopa de Calabaza
PUMPKIN SOUP

Pumpkin soup always reminds me of Halloween. As a child growing up in Miami, I remember going door to door with my entire family. We kids would approach each door and knock. As the doors would open, a choir of Cuban parents, grandparents, aunts, and uncles (all behind us) would chant in unison, "Trico-tree!" (Cuban for "Trick or Treat"). We'd be sure to say it very loudly, in case the entire neighborhood did not hear. Thank God we were in disguise!

This pumpkin soup, now a fall classic at my house, is wonderfully creamy and delicious, a perfect treat for adults and children alike. Try it this Halloween before your own "trico-treeing." It goes really well with Pan Frito *(Fried Cuban Bread) (page 81).*

SERVES 6 TO 8

4 cups chicken stock

3 cups cubed *calabaza* or pumpkin

1 bay leaf

1 tablespoon butter

2 garlic cloves, minced

½ cup diced onion

¼ cup diced celery

¼ cup diced carrots

½ teaspoon ground nutmeg

½ cup heavy cream

1 teaspoon salt, plus more as needed

½ teaspoon white pepper, plus more as needed

Bring the chicken stock to a boil in a large pot over medium heat. Add the *calabaza* and bay leaf. Reduce the heat to low, cover the pot, and cook the soup for 45 minutes to 1 hour, until the *calabaza* is fork-tender. Remove and discard the bay leaf.

Melt the butter in a large frying pan over medium heat. Add the garlic, onion, celery, and carrots, and sauté for 10 to 15 minutes, until the carrots are soft. Add the nutmeg, cream, salt, and pepper, and stir well. Add this mixture to the soup and stir to combine.

Using an immersion blender, or working in small batches with a standard blender or food processor, purée the soup until it is creamy. Return the soup to the pot, taste, and adjust the seasonings, as necessary.

Ajiaco
MEAT AND VEGETABLE STEW

Ok, let me be perfectly honest: I never ate Ajiaco, *this hearty meat and vegetable stew, until I was well into my adult years. It isn't because it's not good. In fact, most Cubans love it (apparently, it's Cuba's national dish). As a child, I just didn't like the name, which, when pronounced correctly, sounds like Ah-jee-you-ko. I'll admit it, to me, it doesn't sound very appetizing. In fact, when we were growing up, my brother and I used to call it "yuck soup" because the word* Ajiaco *reminded us of the word "yuck."*

But, since this book is about traditional Cuban cuisine, and this is my mom's recipe, I've included it at her insistence. As every good Cuban daughter knows, saying no to one's mother is not an option. So here's my mother's recipe for Ajiaco, or "yuck soup." I trust you'll be braver than my brother and me and give it a try. After all, millions of Cubans can't be wrong!

SERVES 8 TO 10

1½ pound *tasajo* (salt-cured beef)

1½ pounds pork loin

1 pound flank steak

1 bay leaf

1 (¾- to 1-pound) *malanga*

1 (¾- to 1-pound) *boniato*

1 (¾- to 1-pound) *yuca*

1 (¾-pound) *calabaza*

1 green plantain

1 sweet (black) plantain

3 ears corn

½ cup olive oil

4 garlic cloves

1 medium green bell pepper

2 medium onions

1 cup tomato sauce

½ teaspoon dried oregano leaves

½ teaspoon ground cumin

1 to 2 teaspoons salt

½ teaspoon white pepper

At least 24 hours in advance, place the *tasajo* in a large bowl and add cool water to cover. Soak for at least 24 hours, changing the water every 2 hours. Rinse and set aside.

Bring 3 quarts water to a boil in a large stockpot over high heat. Meanwhile, cut the pork into chunks about 1-inch in size. Add the *tasajo*, pork, flank steak, and bay leaf to the stockpot. Reduce the heat to medium-low and simmer for 1½ hours—the broth will reduce by at least one-third. Skim the top of the stock occasionally to remove any residue.

While the meats cook, prepare your vegetables. Peel the *malanga, boniato, yuca*, and *calabaza*, and chop them all into 1½-inch cubes. Peel the green plantain and cut it into 2-inch-thick slices. Peel the sweet plantain and cut it into 1-inch-thick slices. Shuck the ears of corn and cut them into 2-inch-thick slices. Chop the garlic, bell pepper, and onions or process them together in a food processor; set aside. When the meat has cooked, add the *malanga* and stir to evenly distribute it in the soup. Continue adding each vegetable in the same manner—the *boniato, yuca, calabaza*, plantains, and corn—mixing each in before adding the next. Cover the pot, raise the heat to medium, and cook until all the vegetables are cooked through, 25 to 30 minutes.

Heat the olive oil in a pan over medium-high heat. Add the garlic, bell pepper, and onion, and sauté for 5 to 7 minutes, until the vegetables soften and the flavors are well incorporated. Add the tomato sauce and lower the heat. Simmer for 20 minutes. This is your *sofrito*, an essential Cuban addition.

Add the *sofrito* to the stockpot and stir well. Stir in the oregano, cumin, salt, and pepper. Remove and discard the bay leaf.

Potaje de Garbanzos
CHICKPEA STEW

*You know that old saying "Beans, beans, they're good for your heart, the more you eat the more you . . ."
experience flatulence? Beans may very well be the perfect food. They contain a nutritionally sound protein-
to-carbohydrate ratio that every food would be lucky to possess. But alas, the gas! Chickpeas are particular
culprits. There is no scientific reason that I am aware of, but I've conducted some random, double-blind stud-
ies of my own and concluded that these legumes cause the noisiest gas of all. But don't let that dissuade
you. This stew is divine and well worth the symphony that may accompany it. If you can't find* calabaza*, use
pumpkin or butternut squash instead. In a pinch, I've even used carrots.*

SERVES 8 TO 10

1 pound dried chickpeas,
   rinsed, soaked overnight

½ pound ham hock

1 bay leaf

¼ cup olive oil, plus more as
   needed

1 cup diced onion

½ cup diced green bell pepper

4 garlic cloves, minced

1½ cups tomato sauce

3 tablespoons tomato paste

3 medium white potatoes,
   peeled and cubed

2 cups cubed *calabaza*

¾ pound Spanish chorizo
   sausage, sliced

1 tablespoon paprika

½ cup *vino seco* (dry white
   cooking wine)

1 tablespoon red wine vinegar

Salt and pepper

Arroz Blanco (White Rice)
   (page 82), for serving

Fill a large pot two-thirds full with water and bring it to a boil. Add
the chickpeas with their soaking liquid, ham hock, and bay leaf.
Reduce the heat to low and cook the soup, covered, for 3 to 3½
hours, until the chickpeas are tender. You may need to add more
water during the cooking process—the pot should always be about
three-quarters full.

Heat the olive oil in a pan over medium heat. Add the onion, bell
pepper, and garlic, and sauté for 5 to 7 minutes, until the onion is
translucent. Add the tomato sauce and tomato paste and cook for
another 5 minutes.

Add the tomato mixture to the soup, followed by the potatoes,
calabaza, chorizo, paprika, *vino seco*, vinegar, and salt and pepper
to taste. Bring the soup to a boil, stirring frequently, and let boil for
3 minutes. Reduce the heat to low, cover the pot, and let the soup
simmer for another 30 minutes. Adjust the seasonings, if necessary. Remove and discard the bay leaf.

Serve with a drizzle of olive oil and a side of steaming white rice.

Chicharos
SPLIT PEA SOUP

This split pea soup is comfort food in the truest sense of the word. It is rich and creamy, and it reminds me of my childhood. To be perfectly honest, to me, almost all food is comfort food. I do not eat merely because I am hungry; I eat, and cook, because eating food and feeding others satisfies me like nothing else. I enjoy the process of planning a menu, going to the market to buy the ingredients, chopping, marinating, cooking, and eating—it is all so satisfying to me. I also like things that, like this soup, require some time to cook. Waiting and anticipating is almost as good as that first spoonful. Almost.

SERVES 6 TO 8

1 pound peeled *chicharos* (split peas)

1 bay leaf

¼ cup olive oil, plus more as needed

2 garlic cloves, minced

1 medium onion, chopped

1 small green bell pepper, chopped

½ pound Spanish chorizo sausage, sliced

¼ cup tomato sauce

4 medium potatoes, cut into 1-inch chunks

1 cup chopped *calabaza*

1 teaspoon salt

½ teaspoon pepper

Bring 3 quarts of water to a boil in a large stockpot. Add the peas and bay leaf and reduce the heat to low. Let the soup simmer for about 45 minutes.

Meanwhile, heat the oil in a large frying pan over medium-high heat. Add the garlic, onion, and bell pepper, and lightly sauté for 5 to 7 minutes, until soft. Add the chorizo, reduce the heat to medium, and cook 5 minutes, then add the tomato sauce and cook for another 5 minutes. Set aside.

After the peas have simmered for 45 minutes, add the chorizo mixture, the potatoes, *calabaza*, salt, and pepper to the stockpot. Cook for another 30 minutes, stirring frequently.

Remove the soup from the heat and let it cool to room temperature, to allow the soup to thicken and the flavors to come together completely. Remove and discard the bay leaf. Taste the soup and adjust the seasonings, if necessary. Reheat the soup to the desired temperature and serve with a drizzle of olive oil on top.

Lentejas Campesinas
COUNTRY-STYLE LENTIL SOUP

Lentil soup is a Cuban favorite because it is so hearty and nutritious. In our attempts to Americanize every-thing, we call this lentil soup campesina *or "country style." We believe that because we add some carrots and 'taters to a dish, we should be out steering cattle. Of course, we also add ham, chorizo, and* calabaza; *not exactly what one would call "home on the range," but good, nonetheless.*

SERVES 6 TO 8

¼ cup olive oil

¼ pound cooking ham, diced

¼ pound Spanish chorizo
   sausage, diced

3 garlic cloves, minced

1 large onion, diced

6 cups homemade or low-
   sodium canned chicken stock

½ cup tomato sauce

¼ cup *vino seco*
   (dry white cooking wine)

1 tablespoon red wine vinegar

1 pound dried lentils, rinsed
   in cold water and soaked
   for 30 minutes

1 bay leaf

½ teaspoon ground cumin

½ teaspoon paprika

½ teaspoon ground oregano

½ teaspoon salt

½ teaspoon pepper

2 large white potatoes, peeled
   and cut into 1-inch pieces

3 carrots, peeled and diced
   into ½-inch pieces

½ cup diced *calabaza*
   or pumpkin

Heat half the olive oil in a large stockpot over medium heat. Add the ham and chorizo and sauté for 3 to 5 minutes, until the chorizo browns slightly. Add the garlic and onion and cook for another 5 minutes, until the onion softens.

Add the stock, tomato sauce, *vino seco*, red wine vinegar, lentils, bay leaf, cumin, paprika, oregano, salt, and pepper, and stir well. Bring to a boil over medium heat and continue boiling for 3 minutes. Reduce the heat to low, cover the pot, and cook, stirring occasionally, for 45 minutes to 1 hour, until the lentils are tender. Add the potatoes, carrots, and *calabaza*, and cook for 25 top 30 minutes, until tender. Taste and adjust the seasonings as necessary. Remove and discard the bay leaf.

Caldo Gallego

GALICIAN BEAN SOUP

Caldo Gallego is a substantial and scrumptious white bean soup that originated in Galicia, Spain, and has since been usurped by Cubans and added to their cuisine. I love it because it is the perfect excuse to make a big of batch of Pan Frito *(Fried Cuban Bread)—the soup being the perfect accompaniment to the bread, of course.*

SERVES 8 TO 10

1 pound dry white beans (such as navy, kidney, or great Northern), rinsed, soaked overnight, and drained

½ pound ham hock or shank bones

½ pound flank steak

3 ounces cured pork fatback or salt pork, rind removed

1 small turnip, halved

1 large onion, diced

3 garlic cloves, minced

3 medium potatoes, diced

½ pound Spanish chorizo sausage, sliced

3 tablespoons olive oil, plus more for drizzling

Salt and pepper

2 cups chopped fresh collard greens or turnip greens

Pan Frito (Fried Cuban Bread) (page 81), for serving

Combine 2 quarts water, the beans, ham hock, flank steak, pork fatback, turnip, onion, and garlic in a large pot over medium-high heat. Bring the soup to a boil; boil for 10 minutes. Reduce the heat to low, cover the pot, and cook the soup for 2 to 2½ hours.

Remove the soup from the heat and let it sit for 15 to 30 minutes, so the soup can thicken and the flavors come together. Remove the ham hock, fatback, turnip, and flank steak from the pot, discarding the fatback and turnip. Shred the flank steak and return it to the soup. Remove the meat from the ham hock and return it to the soup. Discard the bones.

Add the potatoes, chorizo, olive oil, and salt and pepper to taste. Cover the pot and let the soup cook over low heat for another 30 to 45 minutes, until the potatoes are fork-tender. During the last 10 minutes of the cooking process, add the collard greens. Taste the soup and adjust the seasonings, if necessary. Drizzle a little olive oil into the soup and serve piping hot with *Pan Frito* (Fried Cuban Bread).

Fabada Asturiana
ASTURIAN BEAN STEW

Every self-respecting Cuban loves Fabada, *this rich bean stew that is a close cousin to the classic French cassoulet. Few, however, venture to make it themselves. It's actually much easier than you might think. All you need to set the scene is a cold night (rare in Miami), a bunch of friends, and a big pitcher of sangria. Obviously, you'll need the ingredients, too. Oh, and don't forget the* Pan Frito *(Fried Cuban Bread). A double batch is essential!*

Some of the ingredients in this stew are quite unique, and may be difficult to find. I have substituted the fabas for cannellini beans many times with excellent results. The blood sausage and ham hocks are optional, and I often leave them out. While authenticity is important in cooking, let's not forget that practicality can be just as tasty!

SERVES 6

2 tablespoons olive oil

1 small white onion,
    finely sliced

2 garlic cloves, minced

¾ pound Spanish chorizo
    sausage, sliced

½ pound *jamón Serrano*
    (Serrano ham), diced

½ pound *lacón* or ham hocks,
    optional

1 pound *morcilla*, optional

1 pound *fabas*, rinsed, soaked
    overnight, and drained

1 teaspoon paprika

3 or 4 saffron threads

Salt and pepper

Chopped fresh flat-leaf parsley,
    for garnish

Pan Frito (Fried Cuban Bread)
    (page 81), for serving

Heat the olive oil in a large, heavy pot over medium heat. Add the onion and garlic, and sauté for 5 to 7 minutes, until the onions are translucent. Add the chorizo, ham, *lacón*, and *morcilla*, and stir well. Cook for 5 minutes. Add the beans and enough water to cover, and bring to a gentle boil. Reduce the temperature to low, add the paprika, saffron, and salt and pepper to taste, then cover the pot, and let the soup simmer for about 1½ hours, stirring occasionally, until the beans are tender. If necessary, add additional water to keep the beans and meat covered.

Remove the soup from the heat and cool to room temperature to allow the flavors and textures of the soup to develop. Taste the soup and adjust the seasonings, if necessary.

Reheat the soup before serving. Garnish with parsley and a drizzle of olive oil and serve with *Pan Frito* (Fried Cuban Bread).

Sopa de Pescado
CUBAN-STYLE FISH STEW

Similar to cioppino, *the fish soup created by Italian immigrant fishermen in San Francisco,* Sopa de Pescado *makes a wonderful lunch or light dinner. Hmmm . . . light. What a concept! Serve this soup with* Pan de Ajo *(Cuban Garlic Bread) and a steaming bowl of* Arroz Blanco *(White Rice) (pages 79 and 82).*

SERVES 6 TO 8

¼ cup olive oil, plus more
   as needed

3 garlic cloves, minced

1 large onion, diced

½ cup diced red bell pepper

½ cup diced carrots

½ cup diced celery

½ cup dry white wine

2 cups canned
   crushed tomatoes

1 bay leaf

1 teaspoon paprika

4 cups fish stock

1 cup diced white potato

2 pounds Mahi Mahi or any
   other firm white fish

Salt and pepper

Chopped parsley, for garnish

Lime wedges, for garnish

Heat half the olive oil in a large, heavy pot over medium heat. Add the garlic, onion, and pepper, and sauté for 5 to 7 minutes, until the vegetables soften. Add the carrots and celery and cook an additional 5 minutes. Add the wine, tomatoes, bay leaf, paprika, and stock, and bring to a boil. Add the potatoes, reduce the heat to low, and cover the pot. Cook for 20 to 30 minutes, until the potatoes are soft.

Heat the remaining olive oil in a large frying pan over medium-high heat.

Season the fish generously with salt and pepper, then add it to the hot pan. Sear for 2 to 3 minutes on each side, just long enough to create a light brown coating on the fish. It is not necessary to cook the fish all the way through.

Break the fish into pieces, add it to the soup and stir lightly. The fish will cook in about 5 minutes; you'll know it's cooked when it is opaque in the center. Taste the soup and adjust the seasonings, if necessary. Remove and discard the bay leaf.

Garnish the soup with parsley and serve with lime wedges and a drizzle of olive oil.

Guiso de Maíz
CUBAN CORN CHOWDER

Nothing warms you up like a hot, steaming bowl of creamy corn chowder. Guiso de Maíz *is just like regular corn chowder, but like all things Cuban, it has a few special ingredients that make it just a little more flavorful and—well, let's be honest here—more fattening. I like to use a sweet ham in this soup, like a glazed or maple ham, but a smoked ham works nicely, as well. If you can't find* calabaza, *use pumpkin or carrots instead.*

SERVES 6 TO 8

¼ cup olive oil

¼ pound ham, diced

¾ pound Spanish chorizo
    sausage, diced

1 medium yellow onion, diced

3 garlic cloves, minced

1 small green bell pepper, diced

6 cups chicken stock

½ cup tomato sauce

1 cup diced white potatoes

Salt and pepper

1 cup diced *calabaza*

Kernels from 6 ears fresh corn

¼ cup *vino seco* (dry white
    cooking wine)

1 tablespoon red wine vinegar

1 bay leaf

Heat the olive oil in a large pot over medium heat. Add the ham and chorizo and sauté for 3 to 5 minutes, until they begin to brown. Add the onion, garlic, and bell pepper, and cook for 5 minutes, until the onion is translucent. Add 5 cups of the stock, the tomato sauce, potatoes, and salt and pepper to taste. Stir well, cover the pot, and let the soup simmer over medium heat for 10 minutes.

Add the *calabaza*, corn, *vino seco*, vinegar, and bay leaf. If the vegetables look crowded, add the remaining 1 cup stock; if there is plenty of stock in the pot, omit it altogether. Cover the pot and reduce the heat to low. Let the soup cook for 30 to 45 minutes, stirring occasionally, until the *calabaza* is tender. Taste the soup and adjust the seasonings, if necessary. Remove and discard the bay leaf.

Note: When this soup is refrigerated, it condenses and becomes very thick. When reheating leftovers, add additional stock as necessary.

Harina con Cangrejo

POLENTA WITH CRABMEAT

Harina is traditional Cuban comfort food. It's really a simple polenta that, over the years, has been gourmetized. (I know, I know, that's not a word.) Cubans have been making this forever—as baby food, or as simple peasant food with a fried egg on top. Not exactly gourmet, right? But with the addition of savory sofrito-infused crabmeat, it's a whole different story. Now we're talking gourmet! Cuban bread is a must with this dish. What am I saying? Cuban bread is a must with every dish!

SERVES 6

Crab

¼ cup olive oil

1 cup chopped onion

3 garlic cloves, minced

½ cup chopped green bell pepper

1 cup tomato sauce

¼ cup *vino seco*
  (dry white cooking wine)

¼ cup diced pimentos

1 bay leaf

Tabasco or other hot sauce,
  optional

1 teaspoon salt

½ teaspoon pepper

½ teaspoon paprika

1 pound fresh lump crabmeat,
  picked clean

Harina

1½ cups fine-ground yellow
  cornmeal

3 tablespoons olive oil

1 teaspoon salt

½ teaspoon white pepper

¼ teaspoon paprika

To make the crab, heat the olive oil in a large frying pan over medium heat. Add the onion, garlic, and bell pepper, and sauté for 5 to 7 minutes, until the vegetables are tender. Add the tomato sauce, *vino seco*, pimentos, bay leaf, Tabasco, salt, pepper, and paprika, and cook for 5 minutes. Stir in the crabmeat and taste to adjust the seasonings, if necessary. Set aside.

To make the *harina*, bring 2 quarts water to a boil in a large pot. Add the cornmeal, olive oil, salt, pepper, and paprika, stirring frequently with a wire whisk. Reduce the heat to low, cover the pot, and cook for another 35 to 40 minutes, until the *harina* is thick and creamy, stirring occasionally to prevent lumps from forming. Taste the *harina* and adjust the seasonings, if necessary.

To serve, spoon the *harina* into deep bowls and top with the tomato-crab mixture.

Tamal en Cazuela
SOFT POLENTA WITH PORK

Tamales are a popular snack and party food among Cubans. They are often sold wrapped in the cornhusks in which they are boiled. In my neighborhood, you could either make tamales yourself or order smaller tamales wrapped in tiny foil packets from your local Cuban bakery. When I was a little girl, we always had tamales at my birthday parties. My mom used to spend hours making them.

Tamal en Cazuela is basically tamales in a pot—a creamy, thick, cornmeal-based soup that is delicious and satisfying. It is really the Cuban version of polenta. And since we Cubans need to add animal protein to everything, this recipe includes pork (of course). Be sure to marinate the pork for at least thirty minutes and up to twenty-four hours.

SERVES 6 TO 8

½ cup fresh sour orange juice, or an even mixture of lime juice and orange juice

3 teaspoons salt

1 teaspoon white pepper

½ teaspoon paprika

½ teaspoon ground cumin

1 pound lean pork loin, cut into 1-inch chunks

⅓ cup olive oil

1 small green bell pepper, chopped

1 large onion, chopped

4 garlic cloves, minced

1½ cups tomato sauce

½ cup *vino seco* (dry white cooking wine) or dry sherry

1 bay leaf

¾ pound Spanish chorizo sausage, coarsely chopped

continued

Combine the orange juice, 1½ teaspoons of the salt, ½ teaspoon of the pepper, paprika, and cumin in a large, nonreactive bowl. Add the pork, cover with plastic wrap, and let the pork marinate for at least 30 minutes, up to 24 hours. Refrigerate it if you plan on marinating it longer than 1 hour.

Heat 2 tablespoons of the olive oil in a sauté pan over medium heat. Add the bell pepper, onion, and garlic, and sauté for 5 to 7 minutes, until the vegetables soften. Add the tomato sauce, *vino seco*, and bay leaf, and bring to a boil. Add the chorizo, reduce the heat to low, cover the pan, and simmer for 15 to 20 minutes, allowing the *vino seco* to evaporate, the flavors to deepen, and the tomato sauce to cook down a bit. Set aside.

Drain the pork from the marinade.

In a separate frying pan, heat 2 to 3 tablespoons of the olive oil (depending on how lean your meat is) over medium-high heat. Add the pork and sear the pieces on all sides. Reduce the heat to medium and cook for another 5 minutes. Set aside.

In a large stockpot, bring 2 quarts water to a boil. Add the red wine vinegar, the remaining 1½ teaspoons salt, ½ teaspoon pepper, and the remaining olive oil. Add the cornmeal while stirring continuously with a wire whisk.

continued

2 teaspoons red wine vinegar

1 ½ cups yellow cornmeal

Hot sauce, for serving

Lime wedges, for serving

Reduce the heat to low and continue cooking, stirring occasionally, for 30 to 45 minutes, until the mixture thickens and becomes creamy.

Add the chorizo mixture and stir well. Taste and adjust the seasonings, if necessary. Remove and discard the bay leaf.

To serve, add the crispy pork chunks atop a steaming bowl of this dense, creamy soup. Season with hot sauce and a squeeze of lime.

Harina con Picadillo

POLENTA WITH SEASONED GROUND BEEF

I like to think of this dish as the "trailer park" cousin of Harina con Cangrejo. *It's from the same family, and it's certainly just as good, but it just can't afford the same ingredients. I mean . . . it's cheaper to make. Was that politically incorrect?*

SERVES 6

Picadillo

¼ cup olive oil

2 garlic cloves, minced

1 medium onion, diced

1 small green bell pepper, diced

1 pound ground sirloin or ground round

½ cup *vino seco* (dry white cooking wine)

1 cup tomato sauce

2 tablespoons tomato paste

½ teaspoon ground cumin

½ teaspoon ground oregano

1 teaspoon salt

½ teaspoon pepper

¼ cup raisins, optional

¼ cup roughly chopped pimento-stuffed olives

2 tablespoons capers

Harina

1½ cups fine-ground yellow cornmeal

3 tablespoons olive oil

1 teaspoon salt

½ teaspoon white pepper

½ teaspoon paprika

To make the *picadillo*, heat half the olive oil in a large frying pan over medium-high heat. Add the garlic, onion, and bell pepper, and sauté until tender, 5 to 7 minutes. Raise the heat to medium-high and add the ground sirloin (the meat should make a searing sound when it hits the pan—use a small amount of meat to test the heat; if it doesn't, increase the heat to high for a few minutes before adding the meat). Stir frequently to break up any large chunks of meat, and cook, stirring frequently, for 3 to 5 minutes, until the beef is thoroughly cooked (no longer red). Drain any excess liquid from the pan. Add the *vino seco*, tomato sauce, tomato paste, cumin, oregano, salt, pepper, and the remaining olive oil. Reduce the heat to low and simmer, uncovered, for about 20 minutes.

Add the raisins, olives, and capers, and stir to combine. Set aside.

To make the *harina*, bring 2 quarts of water to a boil in a large pot. Add the cornmeal, olive oil, salt, pepper, and paprika, stirring frequently with a wire whisk. Reduce the heat to low, cover the pot, and cook for another 35 to 40 minutes, until the *harina* is thick and creamy, stirring with a whisk occasionally to prevent lumps from forming. Taste the *harina* and adjust the seasonings, if necessary.

To serve, spoon the *harina* into deep bowls and top with the *picadillo*.

Sanwich Cubano
CUBAN SANDWICH

A meal in itself, the Cuban sandwich is hearty and delicious. It is best to use a sandwich press to make it. In a pinch, you can use a waffle iron or even weigh it down with a foil paper–covered brick or a heavy cast iron skillet when pan-grilling it.

This recipe makes two HUGE sandwiches or three "normal" sandwiches. I am not going to give you exact portions here. For heaven's sake, it's a sandwich; guesstimate a little! These go great with Mariquitas *(Plantain Chips) (page 99) and a* Batido de Mamey *(Mamey Milkshake) (page 216).*

SERVES 2 TO 3

1 (2-foot) loaf Cuban bread, or French bread

Mayonnaise

Mustard

About ½ pound Swiss cheese, thinly sliced

About ½ pound sweet ham, thinly sliced

About ½ pound lean pork, thinly sliced

Thin dill pickles slices

Butter, at room temperature

Preheat a large frying pan or cast iron skillet over medium-low heat or a sandwich press to 300°F.

Cut the loaf of bread in half, horizontally. Remove a little of the bread on the inside of one half of the loaf.

Combine equal parts mayo and mustard (I prefer Dijon) in a bowl and spread the mixture evenly on both sides of the bread. Layer half the cheese on the bottom half of the bread, followed by the ham and pork. Layer pickles on top of the pork, then the other half of the cheese. Top with the top half of the bread, and press the sandwich down a little.

Cut the sandwich into the desired portions and brush the outside crusts with butter. Place the sandwiches on the preheated pan or sandwich press and press down on the sandwich with the top of the sandwich press or a heavy cast iron pan. Cook for about 5 minutes, until the sandwich is heated through and the cheese is melted.

Croqueta Preparada (Croquette Sandwich): This famous sandwich is a Cuban sandwich with two ham croquettes (pages 26-28) added before pressing it down in a sandwich grill.

Pan con Bistec

STEAK SANDWICH

Almost every Cuban establishment serves Pan con Bistec. *Ironically, I've seen a lot of variations in how it is made. One version includes the steak, sautéed onions, and fried thin potato sticks. Another includes lettuce and tomato. Then there is one that includes thin slices of ham. I really don't like the one with the ham, mainly because I don't get it. It's already a steak sandwich! Pick a meat, any meat, and stick to it. But many people like it because it's more. You know the saying, "less is more?" Well, let's just say that saying was not invented by a Cuban.*

This recipe makes one sandwich. If you want two sandwiches, double the recipe, three . . . triple it. You get the picture.

2 tablespoons olive oil

½ cup sliced onion

6 ounce top round, sirloin, or *palomilla* (minute) steak, pounded to ¼-inch-thick

Garlic powder

Salt

1 (3-ounce) piece Cuban bread (about a third of a 2-foot loaf), or French bread, split horizontally

Papitas Fritas (French Fried Potatoes) (page 91)

Ketchup

Shredded lettuce

Sliced tomatoes

Heat the olive oil in a cast iron skillet over medium-high heat. Add the onion and sauté for 5 to 7 minutes, until soft. Transfer the onion to a plate and reheat the skillet.

Season the steak generously with garlic powder and salt. Add it to the hot skillet and fry it for 1 to 2 minutes per side, until it is cooked to the desired doneness.

Place the steak on the bottom half of the bread and top with the sautéed onions and any pan drippings. Top with a mound of crispy fries, ketchup, lettuce, tomatoes, and the other half of the bread.

Choripan

SAUSAGE SANDWICH

The word choripan *is a combination of two words:* chorizo *(Spanish sausage) and* pan *(bread). It couldn't be simpler to make. Chorizo is easily found in Hispanic markets, but many large grocery stores now carry it as well. I prefer to use the imported kind that comes packed in (I know, gross) lard in a rectangular tin can. If you can't stomach the thought of opening a can of lard packed in lard, then buy the vacuum-packed chorizo instead.*

MAKES 1 SANDWICH

2 tablespoons olive oil

½ cup sliced onion

¼ pound Spanish chorizo sausage, cut diagonally into ½-inch slices

1 (3-ounce) piece Cuban or French bread, about 8-inches long, split horizontally

Heat the olive oil in a heavy cast iron skillet over medium-high heat. Add the onion and sauté for 5 to 7 minutes, until translucent. Add the chorizo and cook for 5 to 7 minutes, stirring frequently. Chorizo is precooked and can be eaten straight from the package, but I like mine cooked until the edges are a little brown and crispy.

Cut the bread in half horizontally, and layer the bottom half with chorizo slices and onions. You may also want to brush a little of the fat rendered from the chorizo onto the top half of the bread. But that would be a really horrible thing to do, wouldn't it? . . . Do it! Do it!

Calle Ocho/Miami Sandwich

CUBAN CLUB SANDWICH

The Calle Ocho *or* Miami Sandwich, *was created by a local Cuban restaurant located on Miami's 8th Street,* Calle Ocho *in Spanish. This sandwich is a blatant attempt to copy the classic American club sandwich! Covering it up is useless. We simply put a club sandwich on Cuban bread and voilà! The* Calle Ocho *sandwich is born. We really should be ashamed of ourselves! But alas, we are not. Truth be told, the sandwich tastes much better on Cuban bread. Serve this sandwich with some plantain chips and a* Materva *(see page 209)!*

MAKES 2 HUGE SANDWICHES OR 3 "NORMAL" SIZE SANDWICHES

1 (2-foot) loaf Cuban bread or French bread

Mayonnaise

Mustard

About ½ pound Swiss cheese, thinly sliced

About ½ pound sweet ham, thinly sliced

About ½ pound turkey breast, thinly sliced

8 slices bacon, cooked until crispy

Thinly sliced tomatoes

Shredded lettuce

Butter, at room temperature

Preheat a large frying pan over medium-low heat or a sandwich press to 300°F.

Cut the loaf of bread in half, horizontally. Remove a little of the bread on the inside of one half of the bread.

Combine equal parts mayo and mustard (I prefer Dijon) in a bowl and spread the mixture evenly on both sides of the bread. Layer half the cheese on the bottom half of the bread followed by the ham and turkey. Layer the bacon on top of the turkey, then the tomato. Top with the shredded lettuce, the remaining half of the cheese, and the top half of the bread. Press the sandwich down a little.

Cut the sandwich into the desired portions and brush the outside of each sandwich with butter. Place the sandwich(es) on the grill and press down on the sandwich with the top of the sandwich grill or another pan. Cook for about 5 minutes, until the sandwich is heated through and the cheese is melted.

Medianoche
MIDNIGHT SANDWICH

A medianoche, or midnight sandwich, is very similar to a Cuban sandwich. The only real difference is the bread that is used to make it. A medianoche, so named because it was usually enjoyed after a long night of clubbing, is made using a soft egg roll that is long like a hoagie and a little sweet. These can be found at Hispanic markets or Cuban bakeries. At regular supermarkets, look for a long (think hot dog bun, but wider) egg roll that is a little shiny on top.

MAKES 1 SANDWICH

1 (2-ounce) *medianoche* roll or other sweet, eggy roll

Mayonnaise

Mustard

2 to 4 slices dill pickles

4 slices Swiss cheese

4 slices sweet ham

4 thin slices roast pork

Butter, at room temperature

Preheat a large frying pan over medium-low heat or a sandwich press to 300°F.

Cut the roll in half horizontally and spread mayonnaise on one half and mustard on the other. Place the pickles across the bottom half of the bread and top with 2 slices of cheese. Layer the ham, pork, remaining 2 slices of Swiss cheese, and the top half of the bread.

Brush the outside of the sandwich with butter, then place it on the sandwich press or preheated skillet and press down with the top of the sandwich press or a heavy cast iron pan. Cook for 5 to 7 minutes, until the sandwich is heated through and the cheese is melted.

Elena Ruz Sandwich

I've often wondered about this Elena Ruz person. Who was she? Why was a sandwich named after her? And why does it have such an odd combination of ingredients—with cream cheese, strawberry preserves, and turkey? Was she pregnant? I had to find out. So I did what any normal person would—I Googled her. Turns out, she lived in Cuba, where she would frequent a restaurant called El Caramelo. She requested that her sandwich be made in this particular way so often, they put it on the menu and named it after her. (I never found out if she was knocked up! I mean . . . with child.)

This sandwich is great hot, but it is also quite good at room temperature. Be sure to serve it with some Mariquitas (Fried Plantain Chips) (page 99) on the side.

SERVES 1

1 ounce cream cheese,
  at room temperature

2 slices white bread

1 tablespoon strawberry
  preserves

3 ounces shaved turkey breast

Preheat a sandwich grill or toaster oven to 350°F.

Spread the cream cheese on one slice of bread and the strawberry preserves on the other. Layer the turkey slices in between.

Place the sandwich in the sandwich press or wrap it in foil and heat it in the toaster oven for 3 to 5 minutes, until heated through.

Frita Cubana
CUBAN HAMBURGER

Fritas, *the Cuban equivalent of the hamburger, have the same effect as Krispy Kreme doughnuts—you can't eat just one. This recipe calls for ground chorizo. While some Hispanic markets sell chorizo already ground, you can easily make this by removing the casings, cutting the chorizo into small pieces, and blitzing it in a food processor. Make sure the chorizo is at room temperature before you do this; it just makes the whole process easier. Traditionally, a mound of thin, crispy fries is placed on top of each* frita, *just before adding the bun.*

MAKES 10 TO 12 FRITAS

¼ cup half-and-half or evaporated milk

¼ cup fresh white bread crumbs

1¼ teaspoon *pimentón dulce* or sweet paprika

2 tablespoons Worcestershire sauce

2 tablespoons chili sauce or ketchup

1 egg, beaten

1 pound lean ground beef

½ pound ground Spanish chorizo sausage

½ teaspoon salt

½ teaspoon pepper

3 tablespoons olive oil

10 to 12 small, round potato or soft dinner rolls, warm

Ketchup

Mayonnaise

Papitas Fritas (French Fried Potatoes) (page 91)

Combine the half-and-half, bread crumbs, *pimentón dulce*, Worcestershire sauce, and chili sauce in a bowl. Add the egg and stir.

In another bowl, combine the beef, chorizo, salt, and pepper. Add the half-and-half mixture and combine by lightly kneading the ingredients with your hands.

Divide the meat into 10 or 12 equally sized balls; flatten each to about a ½-inch-thickness.

Heat the oil in a cast iron skillet over medium-high heat. Add the meat patties and fry for 5 to 7 minutes per side, until the burgers are cooked to your desired doneness.

Place each burger inside a soft warm roll and top with a little ketchup and mayonnaise.

Serve with a *ton* of thin, crispy fries. Then eat just one *frita.*

Just kidding!

Pan con Lechón

ROAST PORK SANDWICH

Pan con lechón *was invented because Cubans never knew what to do with leftover pork. You see, Cubans love to roast whole pigs. It's a kind of "prove your manhood" thing, so it is done often. The day after one particular pork fest, people bought loaves of Cuban bread, made* mojo criollo *(garlic sauce), and voilà! The* pan con lechón *was born! These sandwiches are so good, you no longer need to roast a whole pig to get one. You can order one anywhere, although they are still best when made with leftover roast pig.*

SERVES 1

1 (3-ounce) piece Cuban or French bread, about 8-inches long, split horizontally

¼ cup *Mojo Criollo* (page 93)

½ to ¾ pound roast pork, heated

Thinly sliced onion

Place the bread in a warm oven for a few minutes just to heat it through (not toast).

Spread *Mojo Criollo* on each side of the bread. Add the pork, then the onion, and the top half of the bread. Serve immediately.

Acompañamientos y Ensaladas

SIDES AND SALADS

If you thought that Cuban side dishes consist mainly of fried plantains . . . you would be right, with a few exceptions, of course. Come on, you didn't think this chapter would be about baby artichokes and Brussels sprouts, did you?

I'll admit, we do love our plantains, and with so many different ways to enjoy them, who can blame us? Usually we fry them—*Mariquitas* (Plantain Chips), *Tostones* (Fried Green Plantains), and *Maduros* (Fried Sweet Plantains) all involve deep frying. On occasion, we will boil or steam plantains, such as when someone has high cholesterol but just can't part with his plantains. But that is not the preferred way of cooking them, and it's usually frowned upon. Especially by the person to whom they are being served.

We do eat side dishes other than plantains. Potatoes, for instance. We have been known to boil potatoes (we don't usually mash them) and serve them drizzled with garlic oil and parsley. Still, we prefer our potatoes fried (*papitas fritas*). *Yuca* is often boiled and topped with olive oil and garlic. Of course, like all other things Cuban, it can also be fried. Can you sense an underlying theme here?

But wait! I just remembered something we don't always fry. It's *malanga*, a root vegetable that is usually boiled and puréed. So there, you see? We don't fry everything. Of course, puréed *malanga* is almost exclusively eaten when someone is sick. (I don't know why). Otherwise, it, too, is fried. So basically, we fry just about everything. Hey, no one said this was a diet book. So, dust off your old "Fry Daddy" and get cooking!

There is no denying that Cubans are genetically predisposed to consuming large quantities of carbohydrates. While we do love our starchy root vegetables and Cuban bread, no meal is complete without rice. Rice is the mainstay, the foundation, the *life force,* if you will, of Cuban cuisine. Rice is a nonnegotiable part of our everyday meals. Sure, we've tried to reduce our intake of this big "bad carb." We have even attempted, in vain, to eliminate it altogether. But what would a big bowl of black beans be without this tasty grain we call *rice*? Well, I'll tell you. . . . Just a sad, old, lonely bowl of black beans, devoid of any real culinary value. The solitary beans—uneaten and unappreciated—would meander through life aimlessly, without purpose or hope. Now, we wouldn't do that to an innocent legume, would we? I think not!

Cuban salads are akin to all other types of Cuban cuisine—wholesome and filling. You won't hear a Cuban woman claim to be starving, then order something like, "Endive salad, no dressing." Can you imagine? Just bury your head in a patch of grass, why don't you?! It's not that we are constantly eating, but when we do eat, we *eat*! I think I would rather spend most of the day fasting and have one respectable meal, than eat like a bird all day long. Listen, I am not espousing any particular diet here, and I realize that what I am saying goes against every magazine article written on dieting within the last decade. I understand that, according to most nutritionists and personal trainers, we should eat five or six small meals a day. But I'll tell you what: one piece of string cheese and five almonds does not constitute a meal! Neither does one ounce of turkey and four pretzels. Hey, how about half a peach and a quarter-cup of cottage cheese? Forget it. Let me starve or eat crow (which contains substantially more protein). Who came up with this stuff anyway? No endive salad for me! As part of, and I mean *in addition to*, a good Cuban meal, I wholeheartedly recommend any of the salad recipes in this chapter.

Pan de Ajo
CUBAN GARLIC BREAD

Cuban garlic bread is different from its Italian counterpart in that it contains no cheese and is made using a loaf of Cuban bread. Though Cuban bread is delicious on its own, it is particularly good when toasted and topped with olive oil and garlic. In fact, this is so popular at my house, we serve it with Italian meals as well. We basically Cubanize everything!

SERVES 8 TO 10

½ cup olive oil

2 tablespoons butter, melted

6 garlic cloves, minced

2 teaspoons diced parsley

1 teaspoon salt

½ teaspoon white pepper

1 (2-foot) loaf Cuban bread or French bread, cut into 1-inch-thick slices

Combine the oil, butter, garlic, parsley, salt, and pepper in a small bowl. Let this mixture sit for at least 15 minutes, so the flavors can come together.

Preheat the oven to 350°F.

Spread the garlic mixture on one side of each slice of bread. Place the bread slices on a baking sheet and bake for 6 to 10 minutes, until the butter has melted and the bread has browned.

Pan Frito

FRIED CUBAN BREAD

And the award for Country That Unnecessarily Fries the Most Food goes to . . . CUBA!!!!!

Ok, don't get me wrong—frying is crucial in this recipe to impart that amazing flavor that one can only get from, well . . . oil. Imagine the best crouton you ever had and multiply that by 100! Serve this bread warm or at room temperature. It is delicious with soups or stews or as a snack.

SERVES 4 TO 6 OR 8 TO 10

½ cup olive oil

6 garlic cloves, minced

½ teaspoon salt, plus more as needed

10 to 12 slices day-old Cuban bread or French bread, cut in half if desired

Combine the oil, garlic, and salt in a frying pan that is large enough to accommodate all the bread (if you don't have one, you can fry the bread in batches). Cook over medium-low heat for 7 to 10 minutes, stirring frequently so the garlic cooks but does not brown. Pour half of the oil and garlic into a small bowl and set aside.

Raise the heat to medium. Once the oil begins to bubble, place the bread in the pan, and cook for about 3 minutes. Shake the pan lightly to brown the bread but prevent it from burning. Remove the bread from the pan (do not turn it over) and add the rest of the olive oil–garlic mixture. When the oil starts to bubble, add the bread, white-side down, to the pan and cook for 3 to 4 minutes, shaking the pan lightly to brown the bread but prevent it from burning.

Taste and add additional salt, if necessary.

Arroz Blanco
WHITE RICE

Because the only thing you need to make rice in an automatic rice cooker is the instruction booklet, I will only provide you with the recipe for rice made the traditional way. Don't worry . . . it's easier than you think. Just make sure you don't use olive oil, as it is too aromatic and overpowers the simplicity of the white rice.

SERVES 4

1½ teaspoons salt

1 cup long-grain white rice
(I like Mahatma brand)

2 tablespoons vegetable, corn,
or canola oil

Bring 2 cups cold water to a boil in a medium-sized saucepan. Add the salt, rice, and oil. Continue boiling for 2 minutes. Reduce the heat to low, stir the rice, cover the pan, and let the rice simmer for 20 to 25 minutes, until almost all of the liquid has been soaked up by the rice. Remove the pan from the heat, fluff the rice with a fork, and add additional salt, if necessary.

Note: Most Cubans wash their rice or at least rinse it quickly under cold water before cooking it. We now know that rinsing rice eliminates many of its vitamins and nutrients. Needless to say, my mom still rinses her rice because that's how it was done in Cuba.

Arroz Frito
CUBAN-STYLE FRIED RICE

Many people don't know that Cuba always had a pretty substantial number of Chinese immigrants. In fact, there is even a Chinatown called El Barrio Chino. I couldn't ignore the Chinese influence on Cuban cuisine in this book, particularly since my grandfather was one of the thousands of Chinese who immigrated to Cuba in the early 1900s. This was his recipe for fried rice. I've omitted the MSG he insisted on adding to all his dishes. You can thank me later!

SERVES 4 TO 6

12 medium shrimp

2 tablespoons canola or peanut oil

2 garlic cloves, minced

½ cup diced onion

¼ cup diced scallions

2 cups cold *Arroz Blanco* (White Rice) (page 82), preferably cooked the day before

¼ cup sweet deli-style ham, chopped

2 large eggs, scrambled

2 tablespoons low-sodium soy sauce, plus more as needed

6 slices bacon, fried crisp and crumbled

Bring 3 cups of lightly salted water to a boil in a large pan. Add the shrimp and boil for 2 to 3 minutes, until the shrimp are opaque. Drain the shrimp and set them aside to cool. Peel, devein, and cut the tails off the shrimp. Set aside.

Heat the oil in a large frying pan or wok over medium-high heat. Working quickly, add the garlic, onion, and scallions. Stir continuously for 3 minutes, then add the rice, ham, and eggs. Cook, stirring, making sure the mixture is heated through and the rice is actually frying. Add half the soy sauce and stir so it is equally distributed. Add the bacon, shrimp, and the rest of the soy sauce, and continue frying, adjusting the heat as necessary. Taste the rice and add additional soy sauce, if needed. Serve immediately.

Arroz Amarillo

YELLOW RICE

I just adore yellow rice. It is a great base for so many dishes. I love it on its own, as well as with black beans, which isn't very Cuban of me. Many of you might not know that Cubans consider it very American to eat yellow rice with black beans. It's just never done. But I say don't knock it until you've tried it. Trust me, it's good.

SERVES 6 TO 8

¼ cup olive oil

1 medium onion, diced

2 garlic cloves, minced

2 cups long-grain white rice (I like Uncle Ben's Converted Rice)

1½ teaspoons *Bijol*

4 cups low-sodium chicken stock

Salt and pepper

Heat the olive oil in a large saucepan over medium heat. Add the onion and garlic, and sauté for 5 to 7 minutes, until the onion is translucent. Be careful not to brown the onion. Add the rice and stir well. Add the *Bijol* and stock, and stir to incorporate. Bring the mixture to a boil and cook, uncovered, for 5 minutes. Reduce the heat to low, fluff the rice with a fork, cover the pan, and continue cooking for 17 to 20 minutes, until the rice is tender and fluffy. Taste the rice and add salt and pepper to taste.

Note: If you can't get your hands on Bijol, *you may substitute powdered saffron or actual saffron threads. Also brands like Goya make seasoning packets with* azafrán, *which lend a nice color to rice dishes but also add a lot of salt. If you use these packets it is best to use water as the cooking liquid instead of chicken stock.*

Arroz con Maíz

YELLOW RICE AND CORN

I always ate Arroz con Maíz *growing up, so there is that whole nostalgia factor associated with this dish that I just love. It is a great side dish for* Pollo Empanizado *(Breaded Fried Chicken) (page 165) or* Bistec de Pollo a la Plancha *(Grilled Chicken Breast) (page 168). For a really quick meal, just add some diced ham and serve it alongside a crisp, green salad.*

SERVES 6 TO 8

¼ cup olive oil

1 large onion, diced

1 medium green bell pepper, diced

3 garlic cloves, minced

1 cup tomato sauce

1 bay leaf

2 cups long-grain white rice

1 teaspoon *Bijol*

¼ cup *vino seco* (dry white cooking wine)

3½ cups low-sodium chicken stock

1 cup canned corn (not creamed), drained

Salt and pepper

Heat the olive oil in a large saucepan over medium heat. Add the onion, bell pepper, and garlic, and sauté for 5 to 7 minutes, until the onions are translucent. Be careful not to brown the vegetables. Add the tomato sauce and bay leaf, and cook for 5 minutes. Add the rice and stir well. Add the *Bijol*, *vino seco*, and stock, and stir to combine. Bring the mixture to a boil and cook, uncovered, for 5 minutes. Reduce the heat to low, add the corn, and fluff the rice with a fork, distributing the corn evenly. Cover the pan and continue cooking for 17 to 20 minutes, until the rice is tender and fluffy. Taste the rice and add salt and pepper to taste. Remove and discard the bay leaf.

Congri
RED BEANS AND RICE

Growing up, I was always terribly confused by the rice dishes Congri *and* Moros *(page 88). My mom, who will not admit it, often used the titles interchangeably, thereby contributing to my confusion. Now that I have written this book on Cuban cuisine, I figured it was time to get a grip on which is which.* Congri *are red beans with rice, while* Moros *are black beans with rice. I think. At any rate, I'm sure you'll enjoy these as much as I do.*

SERVES 6 TO 8

½ pound dried red beans, rinsed, and soaked overnight

1 bay leaf

½ pound bacon, chopped

¼ cup olive oil

1 green bell pepper, chopped

2 medium onions, chopped

3 garlic cloves, minced

1 pound long-grain white rice (I like Uncle Ben's Converted Rice)

1 teaspoon ground oregano

½ teaspoon ground cumin

½ teaspoon white pepper

Salt

Place a medium to large sieve over a large bowl and drain the beans into the sieve, catching the soaking water in the bowl underneath. Use a measuring cup to measure the soaking water as you transfer it to a large pot. Add additional water, if necessary, to equal 5 cups. Add the beans and bay leaf and bring the water to a boil over high heat.

Reduce the heat to low, cover the pot, and let the beans simmer for about 2 hours, until they are fork-tender. Let the beans cool to room temperature, then drain them, reserving 3 cups of their cooking liquid. Remove and discard the bay leaf. Set aside.

Cook the bacon in the same pot over medium heat until it is crisp, 5 to 7 minutes. Transfer the bacon to a plate and set aside. Discard half the rendered fat, then add half the olive oil, the bell pepper, onions, and garlic, and sauté for 5 to 7 minutes, until the vegetables are soft and caramelized. Add the rice, the 3 cups reserved liquid, and the oregano, cumin, pepper, and salt to taste, and bring to a boil; boil for 5 minutes.

Meanwhile, combine the beans with the remaining olive oil in a bowl and season with salt to taste. Add to the rice mixture, then boil, uncovered, for 10 minutes, until most of the water is absorbed by the rice. Add the bacon and stir to distribute. Reduce the heat to low, cover the pot, and let the beans and rice simmer for an additional 15 to 20 minutes, until all the liquid is absorbed. Fluff the rice with a fork, taste, and adjust the seasonings, if necessary.

Moros

BLACK BEANS AND RICE

This recipe is made exactly like Congri, *except instead of bacon, the recipe calls for pork shoulder or leg. You could use pork tenderloin, just cook a quarter pound of bacon and use the rendered fat to cook the tenderloin.*

SERVES 6 TO 8

½ pound dried black beans, rinsed, and soaked overnight

1 teaspoon salt, plus more as needed

1 bay leaf

¼ cup plus 2 tablespoons olive oil

½ pound cooked pork shoulder or leg, cubed

1 green bell pepper, chopped

2 medium onions, chopped

3 garlic cloves, minced

1 pound long-grain white rice

1 teaspoon ground oregano

½ teaspoon ground cumin

½ teaspoon white pepper

Place a medium or large sieve over a large bowl and drain the beans into the sieve, catching the soaking water in the bowl underneath. Use a measuring cup to measure the soaking water as you transfer it to a large pot. Add additional water, if necessary, to equal 5 cups. Add the beans, salt, and bay leaf and bring the water to a boil over high heat. Reduce the heat to low, cover the pot, and let the beans simmer for about 2 hours, or until they are fork-tender.

Let the beans cool to room temperature, then drain them, reserving 3 cups of their cooking liquid. Remove and discard the bay leaf. Set aside.

Heat 2 tablespoons of the olive oil in the same pot over medium-high heat. Season the pork cubes with salt, then add them to the pot and cook over medium heat 5 to 7 minutes, until the pork browns and renders most of its fat. Discard half the fat, then add 2 tablespoons of the olive oil, the bell pepper, onions, and garlic, and sauté for 5 to 7 minutes, until the vegetables are soft and caramelized. Add the rice, the 3 cups reserved liquid, the oregano, cumin, and pepper, and bring to a boil; boil for 5 minutes.

Meanwhile, combine the beans with the remaining 2 tablespoons of olive oil and season with salt to taste. Add to the rice mixture and continue boiling, uncovered, for 10 minutes, until most of the water is absorbed by the rice. Reduce the heat to low, add the pork, and mix to distribute. Cover the pot, and let the beans and rice simmer for an additional 15 to 20 minutes, until all the liquid is absorbed. Fluff the rice with a fork, taste, and adjust the seasonings, if necessary.

Note: Look for beans that are uniform in size and color. When selecting black beans, the deeper the color, the richer the taste. Dry beans can also be cooked more quickly in a pressure cooker—just follow the manufacturer's directions.

Arroz Amarillo con Vegetales
YELLOW RICE WITH VEGETABLES

This is a great way to sneak some real vegetables into your diet. Let's face it, the Cuban idea of vegetables—starchy root vegetables or plantains (which are actually a fruit)—hardly qualify. Granted, the vegetables in this rice aren't exactly plentiful, but hey, it's a start. You can always add more if you feel the need.

SERVES 6 TO 8

¼ cup olive oil

1 large onion, coarsely chopped

1 large green bell pepper, coarsely chopped

3 garlic cloves, minced

1 cup tomato sauce

1 bay leaf

2 cups long-grain white rice (I like Uncle Ben's Converted Rice)

1½ teaspoons *Bijol*

¼ cup *vino seco* (dry white cooking wine)

4 cups low-sodium chicken stock

½ cup canned corn (not creamed), drained

½ cup frozen peas

½ cup diced fresh carrots, boiled for 3 minutes

Salt and pepper

Heat the olive oil in a large saucepan over medium heat. Add the onion, bell pepper, and garlic, and sauté for 5 to 7 minutes, until the onion is translucent. Be careful not to brown the vegetables. Add the tomato sauce and bay leaf and cook for 5 minutes. Add the rice and stir well. Add the *Bijol*, *vino seco*, and stock, and stir to incorporate. Bring the mixture to a boil and cook, uncovered, for 5 minutes. Reduce the heat to low, add the corn, peas, and carrots. Fluff the rice with a fork, making sure to distribute the vegetables evenly. Cover the pan, and continue cooking for 17 to 20 minutes, until the rice is tender and fluffy. Taste the rice and add salt and pepper to taste. Remove and discard the bay leaf.

Papitas Fritas
FRENCH FRIED POTATOES

You just won't be able to get enough of these divinely crispy fries, and neither will anyone you make them for, so make sure you have plenty of spuds. You might even consider taking a trip to Idaho to stock up. . . . If you have a mandoline (French-style slicer), this is the perfect time to use it.

SERVES 4 TO 6

2 tablespoons sea salt, plus more for serving

2 to 3 cups corn oil

4 to 6 large red potatoes

Fill a large bowl with cold water, then stir in 2 tablespoons salt.

Heat 3 to 4 inches of oil to 375°F in a large, heavy pot over medium-high heat.

While the oil heats, peel the potatoes, then cut them into ¼-inch slices. Place the slices in the cold water. Working with a stack of 3 or 4 potato slices, cut them into thin sticks, about ⅛-inch wide. Return the sticks to the cold water.

Drop a small piece of potato into the oil to see if it is hot enough to begin cooking. If the oil sizzles around the potato, it is ready. You'll be frying the potatoes in batches, so remove one-third of the potatoes from the water and dry them *thoroughly*. Carefully add the potatoes to the oil and fry them for 7 to 10 minutes, until they are crispy. Make sure you keep an eye on them, or they will burn. Turn the potatoes frequently to prevent them from sticking together. Transfer the fried potatoes to a paper towel–lined plate and sprinkle them generously with salt. Continue with the remaining potatoes.

Serve immediately.

Yuca con Mojo Criollo

YUCCA WITH GARLIC SAUCE

This is a Christmas Eve (Noche Buena) *staple at our house, and most other Cuban households. In addition to beans and rice, of course. Yuca (yucca in English) is a unique and mildly flavored root vegetable that stands up very well to the tangy savory mojo, or garlic sauce. My recipe calls for fresh yucca, but frozen is just as good and easier to find at most markets.*

Mojo Criollo is essentially Cuban ketchup. We use this stuff on everything. Traditionally we serve it over hot yucca, but it is awesome with Mariquitas *(page 99) and a must with* Pierna Asada *(Roast Pork Leg) (page 132). Store-bought rotisserie chicken is actually edible with this stuff, as are plain boiled potatoes. I also eat it with leftover pork and Cuban bread when making sandwiches like* Pan con Lechón *(page 74). Make a double batch and keep it on hand. It reheats well and adds enormous flavor to the blandest of foods.*

SERVES 4

Yuca

3 large or 4 medium *yucas* (about 2 pounds), peeled and cut into 3-inch chunks, or 1 (2.5-pound) bag frozen *yuca*

Salt

Mojo Criollo

½ cup olive oil

10 to 12 garlic cloves, minced

1 medium yellow onion, grated

2 teaspoons salt

½ teaspoon white pepper

¾ cup sour orange juice, or a mixture of equal parts lime juice and orange juice

To make the yuca, fill a large pot with water, add the yuca and salt to taste, and bring to a boil. Boil, uncovered, for 5 minutes, then reduce the heat to medium-low and cover. Cook for 45 minutes to 1 hour, until the yuca is fork-tender.

To make the *Mojo Criollo*, heat the oil in a medium saucepan over medium-low heat. Add the garlic, onion, salt, and pepper and sauté for 10 to 15 minutes. Remove from the heat and add the orange juice. Set aside to cool to room temperature.

Drain the yuca and serve it hot, with *Mojo Criollo*.

Note: The mojo *will keep for up to a week, covered and refrigerated.*

Platanitos Maduros

FRIED SWEET PLANTAINS

There is nothing to this recipe, and yet it is somewhat complicated. The cooking is not the difficult part—all you do is peel, slice, and fry. No-brainer, right? The key is making sure you have the right plantain—it must be at the perfect stage of ripeness. You can do everything else right—peel it really well, slice it to perfection, and fry it in the finest oil known to man. But without the right plantain, you have nothing! Ok, I know I'm being a little dramatic, but I can't stress enough how the right plantain can make all the difference. So, I suggest going to a local Hispanic market and asking the sales clerk, the produce guy, or any "seasoned" Cuban lady you can find to help you pick one out. My method is not foolproof, but here it is: ripe plantains are—well, not green. They are yellow and black, but mostly black. Basically, a ripe plantain is . . . how shall I put this . . . a rotting plantain. Rotting in that it is releasing its sugars, thereby making its skin dark. So the darker, the better. That's the best I can offer you. If you need more specifics, ask the guy at the store.

very good

SERVES 4 TO 6

2 or 3 large *ripe* (black) plantains

2 or 3 cups corn or vegetable oil

Heat 2 to 3 inches of oil to 375°F in a large, heavy pot over medium-high heat.

Peel the plantains as you would a banana. Because they are soft, the skin will come off easily. Slice the plantains diagonally into 1-inch pieces. Carefully place 4 or 5 plantain slices into the hot oil and cook, turning only once, for 2 to 3 minutes on each side, until golden brown. Transfer the fried plantains to a paper towel–lined plate to drain, and continue with the remaining plantains. Serve immediately.

Tostones
FRIED GREEN PLANTAINS

Tostones *are another variation of the fried plantain theme. Here, green plantains are fried, then flattened, then fried again. Traditionally,* tostones *were flattened with newspaper or a* tostonera, *a special device created specifically for this culinary purpose. I don't use the newspaper for sanitary reasons, and the* tostonera, *in my opinion, is a useless gadget that will just clutter your kitchen. Wax or parchment paper work best.*

The trickiest thing about making these delicacies is choosing the right plantain. My personal favorite is the Hawaiian plantain. It is shorter and uniformly fatter than its traditional Cuban counterpart. They are not always available at regular supermarkets, but small Hispanic markets usually carry them. Using the Hawaiian version makes this recipe a no-brainer—you just can't mess them up. They always come out of the fryer crispy on the outside and tender and delicious on the inside. If, however, you cannot find Hawaiian plantains, then buy a couple of really dark green plantains, peel them, and soak them in salted water for ten to fifteen minutes before frying them. Just be sure to dry the plantains well before frying them to prevent the hot oil from splattering.

SERVES 6 TO 8

2 cups corn oil

3 Hawaiian plantains or green plantains

Coarse salt

Heat 2 to 3 inches of oil to 375°F in a large, heavy pot over medium heat.

Cut about half an inch from both ends of each plantain, then cut each plantain, with the skin on, into 1½- to 2-inch slices. Use your knife to peel the skin off each slice.

Carefully place 4 or 5 plantain slices in the oil; it should be hot enough to bubble around the plantain, but not so vigorously that it begins to add color right away. Fry the plantains for 3 minutes on each side, then transfer them to a paper towel–lined plate to drain and cool slightly. Fry the remaining slices in the same manner, allowing the oil to return to 375°F between batches. Leave the oil over low-medium heat for the second stage of frying.

Once you have fried all of the slices, start flattening them, beginning with the first batch, which should have cooled by now. Place the plantain slices, one at a time, between two pieces of wax or parchment paper and press down with the heel of your hand, flattening the plantain slices to about ¾-inch-thickness. Continue with the remaining slices.

continued

Raise the heat under the oil to medium, and let the oil heat to 375°F. Fry the plantains a second time, in batches, for 2 to 3 minutes on each side, until they are golden and crispy around the edges. Transfer them to a paper towel–lined plate to drain and sprinkle them generously with coarse salt. Serve immediately.

Mariquitas
FRIED PLANTAIN CHIPS

If you have only had plantain chips from a bag, you are in for a real treat. The trick to this delicious treat is to fry them in hot oil immediately after slicing them. Exposing the plantains to air for too long will turn them brown. So you'll need to time the cutting and frying of the plantains well. Since you'll be frying them immediately after cutting them, and you'll be frying them in batches, you'll have to cut a few slices, fry them, and then cut more and so on.

Unlike the previous recipe, the plantains used here are green, making them firmer and easier to cut much thinner. If you have a mandoline, *you can use it here on the thinnest setting. It will save you a lot of time (and perhaps a finger or two).*

SERVES 4 TO 6

3 cups corn or vegetable oil
2 to 3 green plantains
Sea salt

Heat the oil to 375°F in a large, heavy pot over medium-high heat.

Once the oil is hot, peel a plantain and cut it into thin slices, no thicker than ⅟₁₆-inch. Immediately place the slices into the hot oil and fry the plantains for 3 to 4 minutes, turning them occasionally, until they are crisp but not brown. Transfer the fried plantains to drain on a paper towel–lined plate and sprinkle them generously with salt.

Let the oil return to 375°F before cutting more slices and frying each consecutive batch.

Platanos Tentación
SWEET PLANTAIN CASSEROLE

Any recipe with a name that includes the word tentación *(temptation) in it and is made with butter, rum, and brown sugar must be made immediately, no questions asked. So get yourself to the grocery store at once! This divinely rich plantain casserole has even replaced (sacrilege!) the sweet potato casserole at our Thanksgiving table for several years now. It is that good!*

Make sure you use extremely ripe plantains in this recipe—the skins should be black and the flesh should feel mushy when pressed.

SERVES 4 TO 6

3 *very ripe* (black) plantains
4 tablespoons salted butter
½ cup light brown sugar
¼ cup dark rum
½ teaspoon salt
½ teaspoon ground nutmeg
½ teaspoon ground cinnamon

Preheat the oven to 350°F. Butter a 13 x 9-inch baking pan.

Peel the plantains and cut them diagonally into 2-inch-thick slices. Arrange the plantain slices in a single layer along the bottom of the prepared pan. Set aside.

Heat the butter and brown sugar in a small saucepan over medium heat until the mixture begins to bubble. Reduce the heat to low, then add the rum, salt, nutmeg, and cinnamon. Stir well and pour evenly over the plantains.

Cover the pan with aluminum foil and bake for 15 minutes.

Remove the dish from the oven, remove the foil, and flip the plantain slices over. Cover the dish with foil and bake for another 15 minutes.

Remove the foil and bake for 10 minutes to brown the top. Serve immediately.

Fufú de Platano

GREEN PLANTAIN HASH

Fufú, the accent is on the second u. Say it with me—Fufú. Come on, again—Fufú! Isn't that the best word? I couldn't wait for the day my mom would make this dish just so I could hear her say it. I would ask her over and over again: "What's for dinner?" Then my brother would ask her, and we would ask my grandmother, and then my dad. I still think it's funny. Pretty immature, huh? I know; it keeps me young. But funny as it may sound, Fufú has the most unique flavor and texture of almost any Cuban dish. It is comforting like mashed potatoes, yet substantially heartier and more savory.

SERVES 4 TO 6

4 green plantains, peeled and cut into slices

⅓ cup olive oil

1 pound ham steak, cubed

1 medium onion, chopped

3 garlic cloves, minced

1 medium red bell pepper, chopped

½ teaspoon paprika

½ teaspoon salt

½ teaspoon pepper

Fill a large pot with water, add the plantain slices, and bring to a boil. Let the plantains boil for 40 to 45 minutes, until tender. Drain the plantains and set them aside.

Heat the olive oil in a large frying pan over medium-high heat. Add the ham and cook for about 3 minutes. Add the onion, garlic, and bell pepper, and reduce the heat to medium. Cook for 5 to 7 minutes, until the onion is translucent. Add the plantains and mash them into the onion/ham mixture with the back of a wooden spoon or a large fork. Add the paprika, salt, and pepper, and continue mashing and stirring, adding more oil, if necessary. Taste and adjust the seasonings, if necessary. Serve immediately.

Boniato Frito

FRIED SWEET POTATOES

You know how people debate about whether pasta was invented by the Chinese or the Italians? Well, there is no doubt in my mind about who invented sweet potato fries—Cubans! Sweet potato fries only became popular in the U.S. in recent years, but Cubans have been making Boniato Frito *for decades. Needless to say, the best* boniatos *in the world are grown in Cuba.*

SERVES 4 TO 6

2 to 3 cups canola oil

2 pounds *boniatos* (sweet potatoes), cut into ¼-inch-thick rounds or ¼-inch-thick sticks

Coarse salt, optional

Heat 3 inches of oil to 350°F in a large, heavy-bottomed cast iron pot. Add the *boniatos* in small batches and fry them for 5 to 7 minutes, just until they begin to turn a light golden color. Transfer the fries to a paper towel–lined platter. Allow the oil to come to 350°F, and continue with the remaining *boniato*.

Just before serving, heat the oil to 375°F, and fry the *boniatos* again, in batches, for 2 to 3 minutes, to crisp them up and make them a deeper golden color. Drain over paper towels and sprinkle with coarse salt.

Yucas Fritas

FRIED YUCCA

The French have French fries. The Cubans have yucas fritas. *And just as French fries taste great when dipped in ketchup,* yucas fritas *taste best when dunked in Cuban ketchup—that garlic-infused ambrosia we call* mojo criollo. *This concludes today's lesson on Cuban fast food. Tune in again tomorrow!*

SERVES 6 TO 8

1-pound bag frozen yuca
2 to 3 cups canola oil
Salt and pepper
Mojo Criollo (Garlic Sauce)
  (page 93), for dipping

Bring a large pot of salted water to a boil over high heat. Add the frozen yuca, then reduce the heat to low and simmer for 40 to 50 minutes, until the yuca is very tender. Drain the yuca and cut it into large sticks the size of steak fries. Pat the yuca dry with paper towels to prevent the hot oil from splattering.

Heat the oil in a large frying pan over medium-high heat. Fry the yuca, in small batches, for 5 to 7 minutes, turning them occasionally, until they turn golden brown. Transfer the fried yuca to a paper towel–lined plate and sprinkle them lightly with salt and pepper. Repeat with the remaining yuca.

Serve immediately with *Mojo Criollo* (Garlic Sauce) for dipping.

Frijoles de Lata
DOCTORED-UP CANNED BEANS

Ok, I'll admit it! Sometimes . . . I cheat! I use canned beans . . . I've even cheated on major holidays like Noche Buena (Christmas Eve)!! What's worse—and I've been a little offended by this—I've gotten more compliments from the "doctored up" beans than from my "slaving over a hot stove" beans! But look, there's no shame in it. If you make a good sofrito, canned beans can taste perfectly homemade. The trick is . . . drum roll please . . . the bay leaf! But not for flavor; for show! Serve these over white rice as a side dish to any meat, fish, or poultry dish. They also make an excellent vegetarian meal.

SERVES 6 TO 8

3 tablespoons olive oil

¼ cup chopped onion

2 garlic cloves, minced

2 tablespoons chopped green bell pepper

2 tablespoons ketchup

3 tablespoons *vino seco* (dry white cooking wine)

2 (15-ounce) cans black or red beans (I like El Ebro or Kirby brands)

1 bay leaf

½ teaspoon ground cumin

½ teaspoon ground oregano

Heat the oil in a large saucepan over medium heat. Add the onion, garlic, and pepper, and sauté for 10 minutes, until the vegetables soften. Add the ketchup, *vino seco,* beans, bay leaf, cumin, and oregano, and bring to a slow boil. Reduce the heat and let the beans simmer for 10 to 15 minutes. Remove and discard the bay leaf. Serve immediately.

Papas con Chorizo
POTATOES WITH SPANISH SAUSAGE

Papas con Chorizo *make a great late night meal. I've heard that it is also a great hangover meal . . . not that I would know anything about that. While this dish might not be able to cure a hangover, it can certainly tame a ferocious appetite any time of day.*

4 medium red, russet, or Yukon gold potatoes, peeled

¼ cup olive oil

3 garlic cloves, minced

1 medium onion, chopped

1 small green bell pepper, chopped

¾ pound Spanish chorizo sausage, casings removed, cut into ¼-inch slices

½ teaspoon salt

½ teaspoon pepper

½ teaspoon paprika

2 tablespoons chopped fresh parsley

Fill a large pot with water, add the potatoes, and bring to a boil. Let the potatoes boil for 20 to 25 minutes, until fork-tender. Drain the potatoes, let them cool slightly, and then cut them into ¼-inch slices.

Heat the oil in a large frying pan over medium heat. Add the garlic, onion, and bell pepper, and sauté for 5 to 7 minutes, until the onion is translucent. Add the chorizo and cook for 5 minutes. Carefully stir in the potatoes; try to avoid breaking them up too much. Add the salt, pepper, paprika, and parsley and carefully stir once more. Taste and adjust the seasonings, if necessary.

Papas Españolas

SPANISH-STYLE FRENCH FRIES

Basically, Papas Españolas *are Spain's answer to the French fry. They are the same, just cut differently. The round shape creates a unique texture with crispy edges and a tender center. They are particularly good sprinkled with fresh parsley and smoked paprika. Make these in large quantities, because they tend to disappear quickly.*

SERVES 4 TO 6

2 to 3 cups canola oil

2 pounds small to medium red potatoes, peeled and cut into ⅛-inch rounds

Coarse salt

Paprika

Heat 3 inches of oil to 350°F in a large, heavy-bottomed cast iron pot. Add the potatoes in small batches, and fry for 5 to 7 minutes, just until they begin to turn a light golden color. Transfer the fries to a paper towel–lined platter. Allow the oil to come to 350°F, and continue with the remaining potatoes.

Just before serving, heat the oil to 375°F and fry the potatoes again, in batches, for 2 to 3 minutes, to crisp them up and make them a deeper golden color. Drain over paper towels and sprinkle with coarse salt and paprika.

Puré de Papas
MASHED POTATOES

Comfort food, anyone? I bet you're wondering what a recipe for mashed potatoes is doing in a Cuban cookbook. I think every culture has its version of mashed potatoes. The Cuban one is pretty basic. Besides, a good mashed potato recipe is essential in any cookbook, and this is a good one. It is mine, after all.

SERVES 6 TO 8

2 pounds Yukon gold potatoes, peeled and cut into 2-inch pieces

4 garlic cloves

½ cup whole milk, warm

4 tablespoons butter, melted

½ cup heavy cream, warm

2 tablespoons cream cheese, softened

2 teaspoons salt

½ teaspoon white pepper

Bring 2 quarts of water to a boil in a large pot. Add the potatoes and whole garlic cloves. Reduce the heat to medium and cook the potatoes, partially covered, for 40 to 45 minutes, until they are fork-tender.

Combine the milk, butter, cream, and cream cheese in a bowl.

Drain the potatoes into a colander, remove and discard the garlic cloves, and return the potatoes to the pot. Using a handheld mixer, beat the potatoes until they break apart. Add the milk mixture little by little while still beating. Once all the ingredients are fully incorporated, add the salt and pepper. Taste and adjust the seasonings, if necessary. Serve immediately.

Puré de Malanga
MALANGA PURÉE

When I was little, I knew I was sick when my mother brought me Welch's grape juice and puré de malanga *on a tray. I have no idea why she brought the grape juice, but the* malanga *is a traditional Cuban healing remedy. Malanga is a root vegetable similar to a potato, with a delicious and distinctive flavor. Once I was older, I feigned many an illness just to get some luscious* malanga *purée and, of course, grape juice. To reheat any leftovers, you may need to add a little warmed milk to thin it out.*

SERVES 6 TO 8

2 pounds *malanga*, peeled and
    cut into 1-inch pieces
1 to 1½ cups whole milk, warm
4 tablespoons butter, melted
Salt and white pepper

Bring 2 quarts of water to a boil in a large pot. Add the *malanga* and reduce the heat to medium. Cook the *malanga*, partially covered, for 35 to 40 minutes, until it is fork-tender.

Combine the milk and butter in a bowl.

Drain the *malanga* into a colander, then return it to the pot. Using a handheld mixer, beat the *malanga* until it breaks apart. Add the milk mixture little by little while still beating. Once all the ingredients are fully incorporated and the *malanga* is the consistency of mashed potatoes, season it with salt and pepper. Taste and adjust the seasoning, if necessary. Serve immediately.

Ensalada de Papas
CUBAN POTATO SALAD

Because I am the undisputed Queen of Carbs, I love potato salad. However, I detest the store-bought, deli-style, preservative-ridden potato salad that most people consume. Potato salad is so easy to make that buying it already made should be a felony. Ok, a misdemeanor.

SERVES 8

3 pounds red potatoes, peeled and cut into 2-inch cubes

4 ounces cream cheese, softened

½ cup mayonnaise (I like Hellmann's)

½ cup Miracle Whip

½ cup minced onion

½ cup diced pimentos

½ cup canned peas, drained

1 teaspoon Dijon mustard

1 tablespoon red wine vinegar

Salt and white pepper

At least 2 hours in advance, place the potatoes with water to cover in a pan over medium-high heat. Bring the water to a boil and let the potatoes boil for 15 to 20 minutes, until they are fork-tender. Drain the potatoes, transfer them to a bowl, and refrigerate them for at least 1 hour.

Combine the cream cheese, mayonnaise, and Miracle Whip in a large bowl. Using an electric mixer on low speed or a fork, mix until the ingredients are fully combined and no lumps are visible. Add the onion, pimentos, peas, mustard, vinegar, and salt and pepper to taste. Mix well.

Add the chilled potatoes and toss well, preferably with clean hands to avoid breaking up the potatoes. Taste the salad and adjust the seasonings, if necessary.

Serve chilled.

Garbanzos Fritos con Chorizo

FRIED CHICKPEAS AND SPANISH SAUSAGE

I like to think of Garbanzos Fritos *as Cuban hummus, just because hummus is so good for you. After all, it is a recommended treat in just about every diet book and health magazine ever written, so I feel really good referring to this recipe as Cuban hummus. Of course, there is that teeny tiny detail about the frying and the chorizo . . . but hey, that will be our little secret. Shhh.*

SERVES 4 TO 6

½ cup olive oil

1 large onion, chopped

4 garlic cloves, minced

½ cup tomato sauce

¾ pound Spanish chorizo
    sausage, cut into ½-inch
    slices

2 (15.5-ounce) cans chickpeas,
    drained and rinsed

1 teaspoon salt

½ teaspoon pepper

1 teaspoon paprika

Arroz Blanco (White Rice)
    (page 82), for serving

Heat the olive oil in a large frying pan over medium heat. Add the onion and garlic, and sauté for 5 to 7 minutes, until the onion is translucent. Add the tomato sauce and cook for 5 minutes more. Increase the temperature to medium-high and add the chorizo (you can remove the casings from the chorizo, if you prefer). Stir frequently for about 3 minutes, until the chorizo renders some of its fat. Reduce the temperature to medium, add the chickpeas, salt, pepper, and paprika, and stir, pressing down on the chickpeas with the back of a wooden spoon to break some of them up. Cook for 5 to 7 minutes, until the chickpeas around the edge of the pan turn golden brown. Taste and adjust the seasonings, if necessary. Serve with white rice.

Ensalada de Tomate y Cebolla

TOMATO AND ONION SALAD

This is a very simple salad that you can throw together at the last minute. It works well as a starter or side dish. The cool tanginess of this salad is the perfect complement to almost any Cuban meal.

SERVES 4

2 medium to large tomatoes, cut into ½-inch slices

1 medium sweet yellow onion (like Vidalia), cut into very thin slices

¼ cup olive oil

4 tablespoons red wine vinegar

1 teaspoon salt

½ teaspoon pepper

Pinch of sugar

Arrange the tomatoes on a plate and top with the onion.

In a small bowl, combine the oil, vinegar, salt, pepper, and sugar. Whisk until all of the ingredients are combined. Pour the dressing over the salad and toss.

Ensalada Cubana
CUBAN-STYLE GREEN SALAD

As I've mentioned before, most Cubans are not big on salads. If avocados are not in season, this simple green salad is usually what is served as a first course. It is light and accompanies the other, heavier Cuban dishes perfectly. It also helps alleviate some of the guilt many Cubans feel about not eating their veggies.

SERVES 6

2 small heads Boston or Bibb lettuce

1 medium red onion, thinly sliced

1 large tomato, quartered

6 to 8 radishes, thinly sliced

¼ cup red wine vinegar

1 teaspoon salt, plus more as needed

½ teaspoon pepper

½ teaspoon sugar

½ teaspoon paprika

½ teaspoon dried oregano leaves

½ cup olive oil

Tear the lettuce into small pieces and place it in a salad bowl. Layer the onion, tomato, and radishes on top of the lettuce.

Whisk together the vinegar, salt, pepper, sugar, paprika, and oregano in a bowl. Continue whisking as you add the olive oil in a slow, steady stream. Whisk until all ingredients are combined. Taste the dressing and add more salt, if desired. Pour the dressing over the salad and serve.

Ensalada de Atún con Papas y Huevos Duros
TUNA SALAD WITH POTATOES AND HARD-BOILED EGGS

This is another instance of an impromptu meal that we Cubans make when our cupboards are empty or when we are just too tired to cook a full-fledged meal. Although it is not a "hot" meal (we Cubans need our hot meals), we make it "hot" with the addition of white rice. It's simple but hearty nevertheless.

In this recipe, I call for Spanish-style tuna, which can often be found in the canned tuna section of most supermarkets. I love this kind of tuna because it is just so delicious. The tomato sauce that it comes packed in is so flavorful; it is reminiscent of a good sofrito. *It is worth searching for. El Palacio brand* Bonito del Norte *is a good one. If you can't find it, you can use water-packed tuna or Italian-style tuna packed in olive oil and combine it with some homemade* sofrito.

SERVES 4

4 medium potatoes,
    peeled and quartered

4 to 5 cups *Arroz Blanco*
    (White Rice) (page 82)

4 (4-ounce) cans Spanish-style
    tuna packed in tomato sauce

4 hard-boiled eggs, quartered
    or sliced

1 medium sweet onion, thinly
    sliced, for garnish

Olive oil, for drizzling

Salt and pepper

Place the potatoes in a pot with just enough salted water to cover them, and bring to a boil. Continue boiling, uncovered, for 20 to 25 minutes, until the potatoes are fork-tender. Drain and set aside.

Fill a small bowl or custard ramekin with hot rice and press it down to mold the rice. Unmold the rice onto one side of a plate. Repeat this three more times with the remaining rice.

Remove the tuna from the cans (do not drain) and divide it among the four plates, placing it alongside the rice. Pour some of the tomato sauce from the tuna cans over the tuna. Arrange the potatoes and eggs next to it, and garnish with onion. Drizzle with olive oil and sprinkle with salt and pepper to taste.

Ensalada de Pollo
CHICKEN SALAD

Before you get excited about the diet potential of this salad, let me clear up a few things. First, this is not a "light" salad of greens with a grilled chicken breast on top. It is a concoction of sorts; a delicious combination of ingredients held together delicately by a massive amount of mayonnaise. Nevertheless, if you have ever had truly homemade Ensalada de Pollo, you will not perceive it as something that could wreak havoc on your waistline, but as comfort food at its best. I do not remember a single party from my youth that did not involve somebody's version of this salad. Of course, my Mom's version, which I give you here, is the absolute best. It requires a little time and a lot of chopping, but it is worth every ounce of effort.

You may wish to decorate the bowl in which you serve the salad by lining it with romaine lettuce leaves and topping it with additional sliced hard-boiled egg, peas, and pimentos.

SERVES 6 TO 8

4 large red potatoes, peeled and cut into 1-inch cubes

1 cup mayonnaise, plus more as needed

1 tablespoon Dijon mustard

1 tablespoon red wine vinegar

1 tablespoon sugar

Salt and pepper

1 whole roasted chicken, skinned, pulled off the bone, and finely chopped

1 large green apple, peeled, cored, and cut into ½-inch cubes

3 hard-boiled eggs, chopped

¾ cup canned peas, drained, with ¼ cup of the liquid reserved

3 tablespoons diced pimentos

Place the potatoes in a pot with just enough salted water to cover them, and bring to a boil. Continue boiling, uncovered, for 15 to 20 minutes, until the potatoes are fork-tender. Drain and set aside.

In a large bowl, whisk together the mayonnaise, mustard, reserved pea liquid, vinegar, sugar, and salt and pepper to taste. Add the chicken and stir well. Taste the salad and adjust the seasonings, if necessary. Add the apple, eggs, peas, and pimentos, and toss the salad with your hands to prevent the eggs and soft vegetables from breaking apart. If the salad looks too dry, add a couple more tablespoons of mayonnaise.

Ensalada de Aguacate
AVOCADO SALAD

This salad is just the right prelude to many Cuban dishes, especially Arroz con Pollo *(Chicken with Rice) (page 158). The coolness and creaminess of a perfectly ripe avocado and the tangy vinaigrette complement the piping hot chicken-and-rice dish flawlessly. Mind you, most Cubans do not necessarily have their salad first, or even on a separate plate. In my house, it's all dished up together, allowing for a bite of salad every so often. Sadly, I do not make avocado salad often, as the ensuing gas it gives my husband has become a major deterrent. Too much information. . . . Strike that!*

Don't cut the avocado too long before serving this salad, as it will oxidize and turn brown pretty quickly. But if you need to cut it ahead of time, squeeze some lime juice over it, then reduce the amount of vinegar you include by about two tablespoons.

SERVES 4

2 tablespoons red wine vinegar

½ teaspoon salt

¼ teaspoon white pepper

¼ cup olive oil

1 large or 2 small ripe avocado(es), cut into 1- to 2-inch chunks

1 medium red onion, very thinly sliced

Whisk together the vinegar, salt, and white pepper in a bowl. Continue whisking as you add the olive oil in a slow, steady stream.

Arrange the avocado on a platter, then top with slices of onion. Pour the dressing over the salad and serve immediately.

Ensalada de Piña y Aguacate

PINEAPPLE AND AVOCADO SALAD

This salad presents a rare combination in Cuban cuisine. While we have been known to mix sweet and savory flavors on the same plate—as with Platanitos Maduros *(Fried Sweet Plantains) (page 94) and black beans—we rarely combine it in one recipe. This unique salad is a real treat and an explosion of flavor. Once you try it, you'll be hooked!*

SERVES 6

¼ cup apple cider vinegar

1 tablespoon sugar

1 teaspoon salt

½ teaspoon pepper

½ cup extra-virgin olive oil

1 head iceberg lettuce, finely shredded

1 medium red onion, finely sliced, soaked in water for 5 minutes, drained, and patted dry

1 large, ripe avocado, sliced

1 pineapple, cut into 1-inch chunks

Whisk together the vinegar, sugar, salt, and pepper. Continue whisking as you add the olive oil in a slow, steady stream.

Line a large serving bowl with the lettuce, then top with the onion, avocado, and pineapple. Pour the dressing over the salad and serve immediately.

Tortilla de Platanos Maduros
SWEET PLANTAIN OMELET

A basic omelet is a foreign concept to us Cubans. This particular omelet—which is actually served best as a dinner or a late-night meal with a side of white rice—is both an homage to my Cuban heritage and an excuse for including the versatile plantain in yet another recipe. Although the combination might sound a little strange, it is surprisingly tasty.

This recipe provides instructions for freshly fried plantains, but feel free to use plantains that were previously fried. Just warm them for a few minutes in the pan before adding the eggs. Your plantains should be ripe for this recipe, soft to the touch, with black skins.

SERVES 2 TO 4

2 to 3 cups olive oil,
    plus more as needed

2 very ripe (black) plantains,
    peeled and cut diagonally
    into ½-inch slices

6 large eggs

1 teaspoon salt

½ teaspoon pepper

Heat about 3 inches of oil to about 375°F in a heavy pot. Add 4 or 5 plantain slices to the hot oil and cook for about 3 minutes on each side, turning only once, until the plantains are golden brown. Using a slotted spoon, transfer the fried plantains to a paper towel to drain. Continue with the remaining plantain slices.

Heat 2 tablespoons olive oil in a medium nonstick frying pan over medium heat. Space the fried plantains evenly on the bottom of the pan.

Crack the eggs into a large bowl, add the salt and pepper, and mix thoroughly with a fork. Pour the eggs evenly into the pan over the plantains. Allow the omelet to cook, undisturbed, for 5 to 7 minutes, until the bottom of the omelet is golden brown and set.

Slide the omelet carefully onto a plate (preferably one that is larger than the pan), flip the pan over the plate, then quickly invert them both, so the uncooked side of the omelet ends up face-down in the pan. Cook for 4 to 5 minutes. Slide the omelet onto a plate, cut it into wedges, and serve immediately.

Note: If inverting the plate seems too complicated, place the frying pan under a hot broiler for a few minutes (watch it closely). You can even leave the oven door open, with the handle of the pan sticking out. This method works just as well, with no egg acrobatics!

Tortilla Española
SPANISH OMELET

Spain's influence on Cuban food should be quite evident by now. This tortilla is additional proof. Often served as an appetizer, it can be eaten hot or at room temperature. Brimming with potatoes, chorizo, and onions, this tortilla is a meal in itself.

SERVES 2 TO 4

2 to 3 cups vegetable oil

2 large potatoes, peeled and cut into ½-inch cubes

¼ cup olive oil

¾ pound Spanish chorizo sausage, roughly chopped

1 medium onion, roughly chopped

6 large eggs

1 teaspoon salt

½ teaspoon pepper

Heat about 2 inches of vegetable oil in a large frying pan over medium-high heat. Carefully place the potatoes in the oil in a single layer and reduce heat to medium. Fry the potatoes for 5 to 7 minutes, until they are a light golden brown. Transfer the cooked potatoes to a paper towel to drain and cool to room temperature. (You can also use leftover potatoes in this, just be sure they are at room temperature before adding them to the omelet.)

Heat the olive oil in a medium nonstick frying pan over medium heat. Add the chorizo and onion, and sauté for 5 to 7 minutes, until the onion is translucent. Add the potatoes, and spread them out evenly, so they cover the bottom of the pan and are evenly distributed among the rest of the ingredients.

Crack the eggs into a large bowl, add the salt and pepper, and mix thoroughly with a fork. Pour the eggs evenly over the potato/chorizo mixture. Allow the omelet to cook, undisturbed, for 5 to 7 minutes, until the bottom of the omelet is golden brown and set.

Slide the omelet carefully onto a plate (preferably one that is larger than the pan), flip the pan over the plate, then quickly invert them both, so the uncooked side of the omelet ends up face-down in the pan. Cook for 4 to 5 minutes. Slide the omelet onto a plate, cut it into wedges, and serve immediately.

Note: If inverting the plate seems too complicated, place the frying pan under a hot broiler for a few minutes (watch it closely). You can even leave the oven door open, with the handle of the pan sticking out. This method works just as well, with no egg acrobatics!

Platos Principales

MAIN DISHES

In Cuban cuisine, the main dish is the main event.
It is the most planned, the most focused upon, and the most talked about of all our dishes. It is by no means the only dish. Of course not! Cubans cook so abundantly, besides the main dish, there is almost always beans, rice, a couple of fried (of course) vegetables, Cuban bread and/or crackers, a dessert, and coffee. But those are all givens. You always have those things. The main course is up for discussion and debate. Everyone has a favorite and everyone has a specialty. The main dishes in this section are everyone's favorites.

There are few things Cubans enjoy more than pork. Wait, let me rephrase that. There is *nothing* Cubans enjoy more than pork. Fried pork chunks, smoked pork chops, pork ribs, pork sandwiches, pork rinds, and—of course, the crowning glory, the king of all meat and the rite of passage to Cuban manhood—*el lechón asado:* the whole roasted pig.

Preparing to roast a pig is a ritual that takes days of planning. Naturally, this is all men's work, and women are not involved—ever! First, the men (Grunt! Grunt!) decide what size beast they need. This is *always* grossly over-estimated. For some reason, these men (Grunt! Grunt!) firmly believe it is possible for one person to consume five pounds of pork in one sitting. Need-less to say, leftovers are the norm.

The men then make their pilgrimage to *el matadero*, a barbaric place where little pigs are tagged and set aside for those who will later feast on them; sort of a death row for swine. The night before Christmas Eve, there is always a long line outside this pig penitentiary. The pig is butchered, brought home, hosed down, and seasoned very generously with garlic, sour orange juice, and spices. Some barbarians even inject Wilbur (my pigs were always named Wilbur, due to my *Charlotte's Web* fixation) with giant syringes—as if it hadn't suffered enough.

Bright and early the next morning, the pig is laid out, either on a home-made barbeque made from cement blocks and an iron grate of some sort or in *La Caja China*, an oven made specifically for roasting whole pigs. This piece of equipment has been the saving grace for many men who couldn't get a homemade grill to work.

As others join the festivities, the men in the family (all self-proclaimed pig experts) congregate around the beast to add their two cents on its preparation. People poke and pull at the pig's skin to determine if the desired crispiness has been attained. More often than not, arguments ensue. As the time approaches for the pig to be served, the guests begin to circle the beast like vultures, plate in hand. All are prepared to grab the piece they have mentally reserved for themselves. God save you if you try to take their share. Basically, they turn into . . . well, animals.

At the end of the evening, the women of the house stand in the kitchen armed with aluminum foil, begging their guests to take leftovers home. But after having eaten close to five pounds of pork, they politely wave off the foil care packages. Who can blame them? The following day, the men of the house (now too tired to grunt) bring back about ten loaves of Cuban bread from the Cuban bakery in the hopes that somebody—anybody—will pass by, craving a pork sandwich for breakfast. I kid you not, there are many takers.

Beef is also very important to Cuban cuisine. A family friend once told me that her uncle's cousin's father, who was a doctor in Cuba (everyone claims to have been a doctor or lawyer in Cuba), said that not eating beef will cause severe anemia. As such, one would be hard-pressed to find a Cuban vegetarian. It would be impossible not to succumb to the pressure of these "experts."

For Cubans, the most common, and quick, beef dish is *Bistec de Palomilla* (Minute Steak), accompanied by white rice and fries or *Platanitos Maduros* (Fried Sweet Plantains). The steak is thin but quite large, often covering a large oval platter. It is garnished with lots of chopped raw onions, parsley, and lime. Other popular dishes include *Vaca Frita* (Stir-Fried Beef), which literally means "fried cow", and *Ropa Vieja* (Shredded Beef in a Tomato Sauce), translated literally as "old clothes." No, I am not making the names of these dishes up, but trust me, they taste much better than their names imply. Both are made with flank steak that is boiled for several hours, then shredded. One of the best things about these dishes is that they can be prepared ahead of time and are often better the next day. Best of all, they are easy to make and really delicious. Of course, I've included them in this chapter—easy and delicious is my middle name. Wait, that didn't come out right.

There are also some amazing chicken dishes in this chapter. Now, I know, you might be thinking, "Chicken? It's so bland, so boring, so . . . not Cuban!" Well, guess what? Chicken, or *pollo*, is the perfect base for the Cuban *sazón*—seasoning, flavor, and spice. Because it is so bland, chicken becomes the ideal vehicle for the abundance of *sabor* (flavor) that only a Cuban cook (or recipe) can add. Trust me, you just can't mess up chicken when you cook it the Cuban way. There are an infinite number of chicken recipes out there, but I'm just going to give you a handful of the best—the ones you and your loved ones (or those you might be enticing to become loved ones) will request again and again.

One that will certainly become a favorite is *Pollo Asado* (Roast Chicken). It is juicy and delicious, even straight out of the fridge the next day. *Fricase de Pollo* (Chicken Fricassee) is a great traditional Cuban dish that is even better when it has had some time to sit, which is why I love to make it when I am expecting guests. If you are trying to be good, diet-wise, the *Bistec de Pollo a la Plancha* (Grilled Chicken Breast) is the best. You'll never believe that being good can be sooo delicious!

Now you may also be surprised to find a significant amount of recipes devoted to seafood in this chapter. It is, after all, relatively healthful and light. But, the truth is, seafood—such as snapper, lobster, shrimp, and crab—are quite prevalent in Cuban cuisine. When I think of Cuba, I think of the ocean. I am a fan of Hemingway's classic tale, *The Old Man and the Sea*, which is set in Cuba's waters. And, of course, those thoughts of the sea lead me to thoughts of seafood.

Even though our culinary heritage is notorious for being heavy and fattening—which, I'll admit, is for the most part true—on occasion, you will come across a recipe or two that could qualify as light and healthful. *Pescado en Salsa Verde* (Fish in Parsley and Garlic Sauce) is one such dish. In this recipe, fish (usually snapper) is covered in a savory parsley sauce—that's the *verde* (green) part—and baked. If you could manage to eat this with a salad, and only a salad, and *maybe* some brown rice, then you would have a *very* healthful and dietetic meal. But who are we kidding? We're gonna eat this with white rice (the horror!) and some fried plantains. Maybe even—I'm not afraid to admit it—some dessert! So there!

Bacalao, or salted cod, is one of my favorite Cuban seafood dishes. When I was growing up, my mom used to make *Bacalao a la Vizcaína* (Cod in a Spicy Tomato Sauce) every Good Friday (for fasting during Lent). It's a delicious and savory dish in which the cod is slowly simmered in a spicy tomato sauce with pimentos, fork-tender potatoes, and peas. At my house, it was served with hard-boiled eggs and *Pan Frito* (Fried Cuban Bread). I'm sure this dish, and many others featured in this chapter, will become traditional staples in your house in no time.

Pierna Asada
ROAST PORK LEG

I love this recipe because it is so low maintenance. I mean, you virtually ignore it once you get it in the oven. Plan ahead though, because you will need to start preparing two full days before you intend to serve this Cuban staple. This pork cooks slowly in your oven for twenty-four hours, after marinating for another twenty-four hours on top of that. So be forewarned.

This recipe calls for a leg of pork, but pork shoulder works nicely too. Hey, why not make one of each? Have a Pork Fest! (Every Cuban gathering is really a Pork Fest in disguise.)

SERVES 10 TO 12

2 cups sour orange juice
  (from 8 to 10 oranges),
  or a mixture of equal parts
  lime juice and orange juice

15 garlic cloves, minced

2 medium onions, thinly sliced

½ cup olive oil

1 tablespoon dried oregano
  leaves

1 tablespoon ground cumin

2 teaspoons white pepper

4 tablespoons coarse salt

1 (8- to 10-pound) pork leg
  or shoulder

Combine the orange juice, garlic, onions, olive oil, oregano, cumin, pepper, and 2 tablespoons of the salt in a large bowl.

Rinse and dry the pork, then rub it all over with the remaining 2 tablespoons of salt. Place the pork in a high-sided roasting pan that will fit in your refrigerator. Pour half the orange juice mixture over the pork, cover it with foil, and refrigerate it overnight, turning the pork over after about 8 hours so both sides have an opportunity to soak up the marinade. Refrigerate the remaining orange juice mixture in an airtight container.

The following day, remove the pork from the refrigerator and preheat the oven to 400°F.

Bake the pork, uncovered, for 30 minutes. Then reduce the heat to 175°F, cover the roasting pan with foil, and let the pig roast for at least 17 hours, or up to 22 hours.

Two hours before serving, remove the foil and increase the oven temperature to 375°F. Continue roasting the pork for 2 more hours.

Remove the pork from the oven and let it rest for 30 minutes.

Bring the reserved orange juice mixture to a boil in a small saucepan. Boil for 3 to 5 minutes, until the garlic softens.

To serve, carve the roast—although most of the time, carving won't be necessary, as the meat will just fall off the bone—and pour the warmed marinade over the pork.

Macarones con Jamón y Chorizo

PASTA WITH HAM AND SPANISH SAUSAGE

You won't find too many pasta recipes in a Cuban cookbook—we're not big on pasta. You can't eat beans with it! But this recipe is the exception. It even includes the other Cuban staple: you guessed it, pork!

SERVES 4 TO 6

¼ cup olive oil

¾ pound Spanish chorizo sausage, chopped

½ pound *jamón Serrano* (Serrano ham), chopped

1 medium onion, chopped

2 garlic cloves, minced

1 small green bell pepper, chopped

2 cups tomato sauce

3 tablespoons *vino seco* (dry white cooking wine)

1 teaspoon dried basil

1 teaspoon dried oregano leaves

1 teaspoon salt

½ teaspoon pepper

½ teaspoon paprika

½ cup heavy cream

1 pound rigatoni, penne, or other short, tube-shaped pasta

½ cup grated Parmesan cheese

1 cup whole-milk mozzarella cheese

½ cup shredded sharp Cheddar cheese

Pan de Ajo (Cuban Garlic Bread) (page 79)

Heat the olive oil in a large frying pan over medium-high heat. Add the chorizo and ham, and cook for 3 minutes, until some of the fat is rendered from the ham. Add the onion, garlic, and bell pepper, and reduce the heat to medium. Sauté for 5 to 7 minutes, until the onion is translucent. Add the tomato sauce, *vino seco*, basil, oregano, salt, pepper, and paprika, and cook for 5 minutes. Reduce the heat to low and add the cream. Simmer for 5 to 7 minutes, until the sauce has thickened slightly and all the flavors have had an opportunity to meld. Set aside.

Preheat the oven to 350°F. Butter or oil a 2-quart casserole dish.

Cook the pasta according to the package directions (do not add oil to the water, but do add salt) for al dente pasta; drain the pasta. Return the pasta to the pot in which it was cooked and pour the tomato/cream sauce over it. Stir in the Parmesan cheese and taste the pasta; adjust the seasonings if necessary. Pour the pasta into the prepared casserole dish and sprinkle the mozzarella and Cheddar cheeses evenly over the top.

Bake for 15 to 20 minutes, until the cheese starts to bubble. Serve with *Pan de Ajo* (Cuban Garlic Bread).

Arroz con Chorizo

YELLOW RICE WITH SPICY SPANISH SAUSAGE

This is a rare one-dish meal. I say rare because Cubans rarely limit any meal to one dish. Of course, this can be served as a side dish, but because it has protein (pork, of course!!!), it could easily be a main course when served with a salad and some Pan de Ajo *(Cuban Garlic Bread) (page 79).*

   Bijol *is a condiment made from annatto seeds, or achiote and is used to flavor and color rice and other dishes. It can be found in most grocery stores and Hispanic markets.*

SERVES 6 TO 8

¼ cup olive oil

1 pound Spanish chorizo sausage, casing removed, cut into ½-inch slices

1 large onion, diced

1 medium green bell pepper, diced

3 garlic cloves, minced

1 cup tomato sauce

1 bay leaf

2 cups long-grain white rice (I like Uncle Ben's Converted Rice)

1 teaspoon *Bijol*

¼ cup *vino seco* (dry white cooking wine)

4 cups low-sodium chicken stock

Hot sauce, optional

Salt and pepper

Heat the olive oil in a large saucepan over medium heat. Add the chorizo and sauté it for 3 to 5 minutes, until the edges of the chorizo slices are lightly browned. Add the onion, bell pepper, and garlic, and cook for 5 to 7 minutes, until the onion is translucent. Be careful not to brown the onion. Add the tomato sauce and bay leaf and cook for 5 minutes. Add the rice and stir well. Add the *Bijol*, *vino seco*, and stock, and bring the mixture to a boil. Cook, uncovered, for 5 minutes. Reduce the heat to low, fluff the rice with a fork, cover the pan, and continue cooking for 17 to 20 minutes or until the rice is tender and fluffy. Taste the rice and add hot sauce, salt, and pepper to taste. Remove and discard the bay leaf.

Arroz con Salchichas

Es muy bueno. ⚹⚹

YELLOW RICE WITH VIENNA SAUSAGES

This recipe is another childhood favorite and, coincidentally, is also extremely affordable to make. According to my mom, when Cubans first immigrated to the United States in the 1960s, they were given rations of foods like peanut butter, pasteurized cheese, and little cans of Vienna sausage, among other delicacies. This quickly became a popular dish in my home.

SERVES 6 TO 8

¼ cup olive oil

2 garlic cloves, minced

1 medium yellow onion, diced

1 medium green bell pepper, diced

1 bay leaf

½ cup tomato sauce

¼ cup *vino seco* (dry white cooking wine)

½ teaspoon white pepper

2 cups chicken stock

2 cups long-grain white rice, rinsed

1 teaspoon *Bijol* (*anato*)

2 (5-ounce) cans Vienna sausages, drained and cut into 1-inch slices

Heat the olive oil in a large sauté pan over medium-high heat. Add the garlic, onion, and bell pepper and sauté for 5 to 10 minutes, until the vegetables are soft. Add the bay leaf, tomato sauce, *vino seco*, and pepper, and stir well. Cover the pan, lower the heat, and cook for 10 minutes. Set aside.

Bring 2 cups cold water and the stock to a rolling boil in a large pot.

Place the rice in a bowl, add the *Bijol*, and stir until each grain of rice has attained a rich yellow hue (be careful with *Bijol*, as it will stain both your hands and clothes). Add the rice to the boiling water, stir well, and reduce the heat to medium-low. Add the sausages to the tomato mixture, then add that mixture to the rice. Stir and continue cooking, covered, over low heat for 20 minutes, or until almost all of the liquid is absorbed by the rice. Remove and discard the bay leaf. Serve immediately.

Revoltillo de Huevos con Jamón y Chorizo

SCRAMBLED EGGS WITH HAM AND CHORIZO

If you've never had a Cuban-style breakfast, you've been missing out. There is nothing like it—the café con leche, the Cuban toast, the revoltillo . . . yum. These scrambled eggs are spectacular, mixed with spicy chorizo, sweet ham, onion, and bell pepper. Whenever I cook with chorizo, I always remove the casings first, but you can leave them on if you want.

SERVES 4 TO 6

6 large eggs

¼ cup whole milk

Salt and pepper

2 tablespoons butter

2 tablespoons olive oil

½ pound Spanish chorizo
  sausage, chopped

¼ pound sweet ham, such as a
  honey or maple-glazed ham,
  chopped

1 medium onion, chopped

¼ cup chopped green
  bell pepper

Cuban bread or French bread,
  for serving

Crack the eggs into a large bowl, add the milk, and season with salt and pepper to taste. Beat well, then set aside.

Heat the butter and olive oil in a large nonstick frying pan over medium heat. Add the chorizo and ham and sauté for 3 minutes. Add the onion and bell pepper and sauté for 5 minutes more. Evenly distribute the chorizo, ham, and vegetables in the pan, then pour in the eggs and cook, undisturbed, for about 45 seconds. Use a spatula to scramble the eggs, and cook for 3 to 4 minutes, until fully cooked. Serve immediately with Cuban bread.

Bistec de Palomilla
MINUTE STEAK

This is the quintessential Cuban beef dish. It is served—usually with white rice and Platanitos Maduros (Fried Sweet Plantains) or French fries and garnished with raw onions and parsley—at every Cuban restaurant, cafeteria, and hole-in-the-wall eatery. Typically, the cuts of beef used are quarter-inch-thin top round or sirloin steaks, called palomilla in Spanish, although you could start with a thicker cut of beef and just pound it thin with a meat mallet before cooking.

SERVES 4

¼ cup sour orange juice, or a mixture of equal parts lime juice and orange juice

1 garlic clove, crushed

4 (6- to 8-ounce) sirloin or top round steaks (*palomilla*), cut or pounded to ¼-inch-thick

Garlic powder (not garlic salt)

¼ teaspoon salt, plus more as needed

Pepper

2 tablespoons olive oil

1 cup chopped onion

¼ cup chopped parsley

1 tablespoon fresh lime juice

Arroz Blanco (White Rice) (page 82), for serving

Platanitos Maduros (Fried Sweet Plantains) (page 94), for serving

Combine the orange juice and garlic in a small bowl.

Arrange the steaks in a shallow, nonreactive dish and pour the orange juice mixture over them. Marinate the steaks at room temperature for 15 to 30 minutes—no longer or they will turn an unappealing grayish hue. Also, because the steaks are so thin, they won't need any longer for the tanginess of the sour orange to penetrate them. Discard the marinade and season the steaks with garlic powder, salt, and pepper.

Heat 1 tablespoon of the olive oil in a cast iron pan until the oil is almost smoking. Carefully fry the steaks, one or two at a time, for about 2 minutes on each side. Transfer the cooked steak to a plate and continue with the remaining steaks, letting the pan return to a high temperature after each steak. Add the remaining tablespoon of olive oil to the pan before frying the third and fourth steak.

Combine the onion, parsley, lime juice, and ¼ teaspoon salt in a small bowl. Garnish each steak with the onion parsley mixture, and serve with white rice and *Platanitos Maduros* (Fried Sweet Plantains).

Bistec en Cazuela
STEAK IN A POT

This meal is made using the same thin steaks as in Bistec de Palomilla *(Minute Steak) (page 138). It differs from that recipe in that, after the beef is marinated and seared, it is cut into bite-sized strips and added to a savory tomato sauce brimming with peppers, onions, and garlic. Cooking the steak in this rich sauce makes it tender and juicy—a steak you do not need a knife to cut. What a concept! Paired with white rice and some* Tostones *(Fried Green Plantains) (page 97), who could resist?*

SERVES 4 TO 6

4 to 6 (6- to 8-ounce) sirloin or top round steaks *(palomilla)*, cut or pounded to ¼-inch-thick

1 tablespoon garlic powder (not garlic salt)

1 teaspoon salt, plus more as needed

¼ cup sour orange juice, or a mixture of equal parts lime juice and orange juice

¼ cup olive oil, plus more as needed

4 garlic cloves, minced

1 medium onion, cut into thin strips

1 medium green bell pepper, cut into thin strips

½ cup *vino seco* (dry white cooking wine)

1 cup tomato sauce

1 bay leaf

1 teaspoon white pepper

Season the steaks generously with garlic powder and salt. Place the steaks in a shallow, nonreactive dish and pour the orange juice over them. Marinate the steaks at room temperature for 15 to 30 minutes—no longer, or they will turn an unappealing grayish hue.

Heat half the olive oil in a deep frying pan on medium-high heat. Add the garlic, onion, and pepper, and sauté until soft. Add the *vino seco*, tomato sauce, bay leaf, 1 tablespoon of salt, and the pepper, and cook for 10 minutes. Reduce the heat to low and simmer, covered, for 15 to 20 minutes, until the sauce thickens slightly.

Meanwhile, heat the remaining olive oil in a cast iron skillet until it is almost smoking. Remove the steaks from the marinade and pat them dry. Fry the steaks for 2 minutes on each side, adding additional oil as needed. Cut the steaks into bite-sized pieces, then add them to the tomato mixture and stir well. Cover the pan and cook for 10 minutes over low heat, so the flavor of the sauce permeates through the beef. Taste and adjust the seasonings, if necessary. Remove and discard the bay leaf.

Vaca Frita

STIR-FRIED BEEF

Ok, technically this dish is what it says it is—beef, or cow, that is, in fact, fried. When I was a little girl, I had visions of an entire cow (live, of course) being lowered into the world's largest pot of sizzling olive oil. . . . Yes, I participated in a twelve-step program to deal with these issues. But like Ropa Vieja *(which means "old clothes") (page 143), the translation of this recipe's name does not do the dish justice. Imagine tender and perfectly seasoned shredded flank steak, fried with onions and garlic until it is slighty crispy. Ok don't imagine it, get out that skillet and start cooking! I love this dish, and I think you will, too. Serve this with . . . I'm not even gonna say it . . . ok, white rice.*

SERVES 6 TO 8

1 bay leaf

2 pounds flank steak

1 teaspoon salt,
plus more to taste

½ teaspoon pepper

½ cup sour orange juice, or a
mixture of equal parts lime
juice and orange juice

¼ cup lime juice

¼ cup olive oil

3 garlic cloves, minced

2 medium onions, thinly sliced

Arroz Blanco (White Rice)
(page 82), for serving

Lime wedges, for serving

Bring 2 quarts of salted water to a boil in a large stockpot. Add the bay leaf and steak, then reduce the heat, cover the pot, and simmer for 2 hours.

Drain the flank steak and let it cool to room temperature on a plate lined with paper towels. Use your hands to shred the beef into long strips; if you shred it along the grain, it should come apart easily. Season the steak with salt and pepper, and place it in a shallow, nonreactive dish. Pour the orange and lime juices over the steak and let it marinate for at least 30 minutes. Drain the beef and it aside.

Preheat a large cast iron skillet over medium-high heat. Add half the olive oil and heat it until it is almost smoking. Add half the garlic and half the steak and sauté, stirring frequently, for 7 to 10 minutes. Add half the onions and sauté for 5 minutes, until the edges of the beef become crispy. Transfer the mixture to a large plate and repeat this process with the remaining ingredients. Serve with rice and lime wedges.

Ropa Vieja

SHREDDED BEEF IN TOMATO SAUCE

I just adore Ropa Vieja—I order it almost every time I eat at a Cuban restaurant. The dish is made by boiling shredded flank steak long enough to make it extremely tender, sautéing it in a savory sofrito-infused tomato sauce, then garnishing it with peas and pimentos. The combination is just divine. I love it with white rice and black beans all mixed together on one plate. The name, which means "old clothes", really doesn't do the dish justice and may intimidate some people from trying it. Therefore, I recommend that you do not translate its name for any of your non-Spanish-speaking friends. Just tell them it is one of those Spanish terms that does not translate well. If they don't buy that, at least wait until after they take a bite to divulge the name of this classic Cuban dish. Serve this with—what else?—white rice, of course! And don't forget something fried.

SERVES 6 TO 8

2 teaspoons salt, plus more as needed

1 tablespoon whole black peppercorns

2 pounds flank steak

½ cup olive oil

3 garlic cloves, minced

1 medium onion, roughly chopped

1 medium green bell pepper, roughly chopped

1 medium red bell pepper, roughly chopped

2 cups tomato sauce

1 bay leaf

½ teaspoon white pepper

½ teaspoon ground cumin

½ teaspoon ground oregano

1 cup *vino seco* (dry white cooking wine)

Lime

½ cup canned peas, for garnish

¼ cup chopped pimentos, for garnish

Combine 1½ quarts water, 1 teaspoon of the salt, and the peppercorns in a large pot and bring to a boil over high heat. Add the steak and reduce the heat to low. Cover the pot and cook for about 2 hours, until the meat is nice and tender.

Heat the olive oil in a large frying pan over medium heat. Add the garlic, onion, and bell peppers, and sauté for about 10 minutes, until the vegetables are soft. Add the tomato sauce, bay leaf, pepper, cumin, oregano, and remaining teaspoon of salt, and bring the mixture to a boil. Add the *vino seco* and continue boiling for 5 minutes. Reduce the heat to low and simmer for 20 minutes. Remove the pan from the heat and set aside.

Drain the flank steak and let it cool to room temperature on a plate lined with paper towels. Use your hands to shred the beef into long strips; if you shred it along the grain, it should come apart easily. Season the steak with salt and pepper and a squeeze of lime juice, and add it to the tomato mixture. Stir to coat the meat with the sauce. Cook over medium-low heat for at least 20 to 30 minutes, to allow the flavors to come together. Remove and discard the bay leaf.

Garnish with peas and pimentos before serving.

Picadillo

SEASONED GROUND BEEF

Picadillo *is a very traditional Cuban dish that is also extremely versatile, because any leftovers can be used creatively.* Empanadas de Carne *(Ground Beef Empanadas) (page 24) and* Papas Rellenas *(Stuffed Mashed Potato Balls) (page 35) are just two recipes that come to mind. Serve this dish with . . . guess! No really, this time I'm not going to say it. (Ok, fine. White rice.)*

SERVES 4 TO 6

¼ cup olive oil

2 garlic cloves, minced

1 medium onion, chopped

1 small green bell pepper, minced

1 pound ground sirloin or ground round

½ cup *vino seco*
   (dry white cooking wine)

1 cup tomato sauce

Salt and pepper

¼ cup raisins

¼ cup pimento-stuffed olives, roughly chopped

2 tablespoons capers

2 medium red potatoes, peeled, cut into 1-inch pieces, and fried until golden brown

Heat half the olive oil in a medium-sized shallow pot over medium-high heat. Add the garlic, onion, and bell pepper, and sauté for 5 to 7 minutes, until tender. Raise the heat slightly, then add a pinch of the ground beef. The meat should make a searing sound when it hits the pan. Otherwise, increase the temperature to high for a few minutes. Add the beef when the pan is very hot and sauté, breaking up any large chunks of meat. Sauté for 5 to 10 minutes, until the beef is thoroughly cooked (no longer red). Drain any excess liquid from the pan.

Add the *vino seco*, tomato sauce, the remaining olive oil, and salt and pepper to taste. Reduce the heat to low, cover the pot, and simmer for about 20 minutes. Add the raisins, olives, and capers. Stir in the potatoes right before serving so that they retain some of their crispiness.

Carne con Papas

BEEF STEW

When a Cuban hears "meat and potatoes," she thinks Carne con Papas. *After all, that is the exact translation. So, while the idea of meat and potatoes would conjure up an image of a T-bone steak and a baked potato for many Americans, a Cuban or Cuban-American will pine away for this savory and delectable stew. Like many Cuban recipes, this dish makes great leftovers and can even be made a day or two ahead. In fact, it tastes even better the next day.*

SERVES 6 TO 8

½ cup olive oil

2 pounds top round, eye of the round, or boneless chuck roast, cut into 1- to 2-inch chunks

1 teaspoon salt

½ teaspoon pepper

3 garlic cloves, minced

1 medium green bell pepper, chopped

1 onion, chopped

2 cups tomato sauce

2 cups beef stock

1 bay leaf

½ cup *vino seco* (dry white cooking wine)

4 carrots, peeled and cut into 1-inch pieces

1 pound red or white potatoes, peeled and cut into 2-inch cubes

½ cup pimento-stuffed olives

Heat the olive oil in a large pot over medium-high heat. Season the beef with salt and pepper. Add it, in small batches, to the hot oil and brown it on all sides. Transfer the browned meat to a plate and set aside.

Reduce the heat to medium, add the garlic, bell pepper, and onion to the pot, and sauté for 5 to 7 minutes, until soft. Add the tomato sauce, stock, bay leaf, and *vino seco*, raise the heat to high, and bring to a boil. Let the stew boil, uncovered, for 10 minutes, until the sauce reduces by a quarter.

Add the beef, reduce the heat to low, and cover the pot. Let the stew simmer for about 1 hour, stirring occasionally. Add the carrots and potatoes and cook for another 20 to 25 minutes, or until the vegetables are soft and the meat is tender. Add the olives and taste; adjust the seasonings, if necessary. Remove and discard the bay leaf.

I recommend you drizzle a little olive oil into each bowl as you serve this delectable dish.

Pulpeta
MEATLOAF

Wait a minute! Do not turn the page or stop reading! This is no ordinary meatloaf. It is not even close to the gray-hued, crumbly, dry brick that perhaps you've sadly grown accustomed to. This is moist and flavorful. It's not even oven-baked in a loaf pan. It is shaped by hand and slowly simmered in a delicious tangy tomato sauce infused with garlic, bell pepper, and onion. The meat is delicately formed around hard-boiled eggs so that when sliced, a tasty surprise is revealed.

SERVES 6 TO 8

1 pound ground sirloin

½ pound ground pork

½ pound ground sweet ham, such as honey or maple glazed ham (see note on page 148)

2 teaspoons salt

1 teaspoon pepper

½ teaspoon dried oregano leaves

1 teaspoon paprika

1 egg, beaten

1 cup dry seasoned breadcrumbs

4 hard-boiled eggs

½ cup olive oil

4 garlic cloves, minced

1 medium green bell pepper, diced

1 large yellow onion, diced

2 cups tomato sauce

1 bay leaf

½ cup *vino seco* (dry white cooking wine)

½ cup canned peas (reserve liquid)

½ cup pimentos

Combine the beef, pork, and ham in a large bowl. Add 1 teaspoon of the salt, ½ teaspoon of the pepper, the oregano, and the paprika. Knead the meat lightly by hand until all of the ingredients are thoroughly combined. Add the egg and half the breadcrumbs, and mix until thoroughly combined.

Transfer the meat mixture to a baking sheet and use your hands to shape it into one or two oblong or rectangular loaves. If this if your first time making this meatloaf, you might try making two loaves instead of one, as it's a little easier. Create a well in the center of the loaf. Carefully place the eggs in the well—all four if you are creating one loaf, or two in each of the two loaves—and fold the meat mixture over them to enclose them entirely in the center of the loaf(ves). Sprinkle the loaf(ves) with the remaining breadcrumbs to create a light coating, then pat the crumbs so they stick. Cover the loaf(ves) with plastic wrap, transfer the baking sheet to the refrigerator, and refrigerate for 1 hour.

Just before you take the meatloaf out of the refrigerator, heat the olive oil in a large pot over medium-high heat. Add the garlic, bell pepper, and onion, and sauté for about 10 minutes, until the vegetables are soft. Add the tomato sauce, bay leaf, *vino seco*, the remaining salt and pepper, and ¼ cup of the reserved pea liquid. Bring to a boil and cook for 5 minutes. Reduce the heat to low, cover the pot, and let the mixture simmer for 20 to 30 minutes.

continued

While that cooks, remove the meatloaf from the refrigerator and let it warm up a bit.

Coat a large, shallow frying pan with olive or vegetable oil over medium-high heat. Carefully transfer the meatloaf to the pan and sear it on all sides, creating a golden crust. It is not necessary to cook the meat all the way through; just enough for it to firm up and remain stable.

Gently place the browned meatloaf in the pot with the tomato sauce mixture. Cover the pot, raise the heat to medium-low, and cook for 45 minutes to 1 hour. Spoon the sauce over the meat occasionally, but do not stir.

Carefully transfer the meat to a large platter and let it rest about 10 minutes before cutting it into slices.

To serve, pour tomato sauce over each serving and garnish with peas and pimentos.

Note: To make ground ham, I usually buy sliced ham from the deli and pulse it in the food processor until it is finely ground.

Albondigas (Meatballs): *Albondigas* are a great variation of the meatloaf recipe, especially for parties. You can make them days in advance, and they are just as good hot as they are at room temperature. These meatballs also make amazing sandwiches. Warm Cuban bread, a few meatballs, a little sauce, and some thinly sliced onions, and you have one heck of a sandwich. Simply use the recipe above—omitting the hard-boiled eggs—and form meatballs of whatever size you want. Roll the meatballs lightly in the breadcrumbs, sear them on all sides, and add them to the tomato sauce, then cook as directed above.

Bistec Empanizado
BREADED FRIED STEAK

Bistec empanizado is like chicken-fried steak without the gravy. I've always been somewhat confused about chicken-fried steak—I mean, is it chicken or is it steak? It's steak, right?! So why not call it steak-fried steak? Or just breaded steak? Are you confused? I know I am. This breaded fried steak, named for what it is, is a Cuban classic. Serve it with Moros *(Black Beans and Rice) (page 88) and* Platanitos Maduros *(Fried Sweet Plantains) (page 94). Most people also enjoy it with a squeeze of lime. Ok, my mouth is watering!*

SERVES 4

¼ cup sour orange juice, or a mixture of equal parts lime juice and orange juice

4 garlic cloves, minced

4 (6- to 8-ounce) sirloin steaks, cut or pounded to ¼-inch-thick

Salt and pepper

Vegetable or canola oil, for shallow frying

4 eggs, beaten

¾ cup finely ground cracker meal

¼ cup all-purpose flour

Lime wedges, for serving

Combine the orange juice and garlic in a small bowl.

Arrange the steaks in a shallow, nonreactive dish and pour the orange juice and garlic over them. Cover the steaks with plastic wrap and marinate them in the refrigerator for 1 hour. Drain the steaks, pat them dry, and season them liberally with salt and pepper.

Heat the oil in a large frying pan over medium to medium-high heat. Place the eggs in a shallow bowl. Combine the cracker meal and flour in another shallow bowl. Dip the steaks in the egg, then in the flour mixture. Repeat this step, dipping the steak in the egg and flour mixture a second time. Shake off any excess flour and gently lay the steaks in the hot oil. Fry each steak individually for about 3 minutes each side, until golden brown. Transfer the steaks to a paper towel–lined platter to drain.

Serve with a squeeze of lime.

Tambor de Picadillo

CUBAN SHEPHERD'S PIE

Tambor is Spanish for drum, and I suppose that if you made this dish in a round casserole, it would resemble a drum. Other than that, I don't know why it is called Tambor de Picadillo. I like to think of this dish as Cuba's answer to shepherd's pie, just with a little more ¡sabor! Serve this with Ensalada Cubana (Cuban Salad) (page 117) and Pan de Ajo (Cuban Garlic Bread) (page 79).

SERVES 6

Mashed Potatoes

3 pounds Yukon gold potatoes, peeled and cut into 2-inch pieces

6 garlic cloves

½ cup whole milk, warm

4 tablespoons butter, melted

½ cup heavy cream, warm

2 teaspoons salt, plus more if needed

½ teaspoon white pepper, plus more if needed

Picadillo

¼ cup olive oil

2 garlic cloves, minced

1 medium onion, diced

1 small green bell pepper, diced

1 pound ground sirloin or ground round

½ cup *vino seco* (dry white cooking wine)

1 cup tomato sauce

2 tablespoons tomato paste

½ teaspoon ground cumin

continued

To make the mashed potatoes, bring 2 quarts of water to a boil in a large pot. Add the potatoes and whole garlic cloves. Reduce the heat to medium and cook the potatoes, partially covered, for 40 to 45 minutes, until they are fork-tender.

Combine the milk, butter, and cream in a bowl.

Drain the potatoes into a colander, remove and discard the garlic cloves, and return the potatoes to the pot. Using a handheld mixer, beat the potatoes until they break apart. Add the milk mixture little by little while still beating. Once all the ingredients are fully incorporated, add the salt and pepper. Taste and adjust the seasoning, if necessary. Set aside.

To make the *picadillo*, heat half the olive oil in a large frying pan over medium-high heat. Add the garlic, onion, and bell pepper, and sauté for 5 to 7 minutes, until the vegetables are tender. Allow the pan to return to medium-high heat, then add a pinch of ground beef. The meat should make a searing sound when it hits the pan. Otherwise, increase the temperature to high for a few minutes. Add the beef when the pan is hot and sauté, breaking up large chunks of meat. Sauté for 10 to 15 minutes, until the beef is thoroughly cooked (no longer red). Drain any excess liquid from the pan.

Add the *vino seco*, tomato sauce, tomato paste, cumin, oregano, salt, pepper, and the remaining olive oil. Reduce the heat to low and simmer, uncovered, for 20 minutes, stirring occasionally, until the tomato sauce thickens slightly. Add the raisins, olives, and capers, and set aside.

continued

½ teaspoon ground oregano

1 teaspoon salt

½ teaspoon pepper

¼ cup raisins, optional

¼ cup pimento-stuffed olives, roughly chopped

2 tablespoons capers

½ cup grated Parmesan cheese

Preheat the oven to 350°F.

Layer half the mashed potatoes evenly on the bottom of a large, oiled or buttered ovenproof casserole dish. Cover the mashed potato layer with all of the *picadillo*. Top with the remaining mashed potatoes. Finish the casserole by sprinkling the Parmesan cheese evenly over the top.

Bake for 20 to 25 minutes, until the top of the casserole turns a golden brown.

Bistec a la Milanesa

MILANESE-STYLE STEAK

This is a delicious twist on Bistec Empanizado *(Breaded Fried Steak) (page 149). It's always amusing to find this dish as a staple on every Cuban restaurant menu. In many ways, it is more Italian than Cuban, but hey, it's served with rice and beans . . . so it's Cuban! Enjoy! By the way, this is great with* Puré de Papas *(Mashed Potatoes) (page 111).*

SERVES 4

¼ cup sour orange juice, or a mixture of equal parts lime juice and orange juice

4 garlic cloves, minced

4 (6- to 8-ounce) sirloin steaks, cut or pounded to ¼-inch-thick

Salt and pepper

Olive oil, for shallow frying

4 eggs, beaten

¾ cup finely ground cracker meal

¼ cup all-purpose flour

1 cup marinara sauce

1 cup shredded mozzarella cheese

Lime wedges, for serving

Combine the orange juice and garlic in a small bowl.

Arrange the steaks in a shallow, nonreactive dish and pour the orange juice and garlic over them. Cover the steaks with plastic wrap and marinate them in the refrigerator for 30 minutes. Drain the steaks, pat them dry, and season them liberally with salt and pepper.

Heat the olive oil in a large frying pan over medium-high heat. Place the eggs in a shallow bowl. Combine the cracker meal and flour in another shallow bowl. Dip the steaks in the egg, then in the flour mixture. Repeat this step, dipping the steak in the egg and flour mixture a second time. Shake off any excess flour and gently lay the steaks in the hot oil. Fry each steak individually for about 3 minutes on each side, until golden brown. Transfer the steaks to a paper towel-lined platter to drain.

Preheat the broiler.

Place the steaks on a baking sheet. Spread 4 tablespoons of marinara sauce on top of each steak, then sprinkle each with mozzarella cheese. Broil the steaks for 2 to 3 minutes, until the cheese starts to bubble and turn a light golden color. *Do not leave your steaks unattended. They will burn!* (I don't mean to be dramatic, but it really would be a shame to go through all this trouble and have it go to waste during the last step, don't you think?)

Serve with lime wedges.

Rabo Encendido
OXTAIL STEW

The literal translation of the name of this dish is "Tail on Fire." As you can imagine, it was another one of those Cuban delicacies I avoided at all costs as a child. I must say, though, I have since developed a certain appreciation for this dish. Oxtail, when cooked properly, is tender and succulent, with a rich, red gravy. It goes without saying that this recipe ensures proper cooking. As do all my recipes. Naturally.

SERVES 6 TO 8

3 pounds oxtails, trimmed of fat and cut into 2-inch pieces

Salt and pepper

All-purpose flour, for dredging

⅓ cup olive oil

4 garlic cloves, minced

2 cups diced onion

2 cups green diced bell pepper

1½ cups diced potatoes

3 tablespoons tomato paste

1 cup tomato sauce

¾ cup dry red wine

¼ cup *vino seco* (dry white cooking wine)

2 cups low-sodium beef stock

1 bay leaf

½ cup chopped parsley

1 teaspoon red wine vinegar

1 teaspoon salt

½ teaspoon pepper

½ teaspoon ground oregano

½ teaspoon ground cumin

Arroz Blanco (White Rice) (page 82), for serving

Platanitos Maduros (Fried Sweet Plantains) (page 94), for serving

Season the oxtails with salt and pepper, dredge them lightly in flour, and set them aside.

Heat the olive oil in a large heavy-bottomed pot over medium-high heat. Add the oxtails in small batches and sear them on all sides. Transfer the seared oxtails to a plate and set them aside.

Reduce the heat to medium and add the garlic, onion, and bell pepper. Sauté for 5 to 7 minutes, until the vegetables are tender. Add the tomato paste and tomato sauce and continue cooking for another 5 minutes. Add the wine, *vino seco*, stock, bay leaf, parsley, red wine vinegar, salt, pepper, oregano, and cumin, and increase the heat to medium-high. Bring the soup to a slow boil. Add the oxtails, reduce the heat to low, cover the pot, and let the soup simmer for 2 hours. Add the potatoes and cook for another 45 minutes to 1 hour, until the potatoes are fork-tender and the meat is falling off the bones. Taste the soup and adjust the seasonings, if necessary. Remove and discard the bay leaf.

Serve with *Arroz Blanco* and *Platanitos Maduros* (Fried Sweet Plantains).

Aporreado de Tasajo

SALT-DRIED BEEF STEW

Tasajo, or salt-dried beef, is popular in Cuban cuisine and has been for many years. Legend has it that the original tasajo *was made with horse meat. I don't know if this is an old Cuban urban legend, but I have heard it more than once, and frankly, it scares me. This recipe, however, is made with salt-dried beef, not Seabiscuit! Keep in mind that you need to soak the beef in water for at least twenty-four hours before cooking to remove most of its salt.*

Serve this tasty stew alongside fluffy white rice, black beans, and crispy Tostones *(Fried Green Plantains), and you just can't go wrong.*

SERVES 6 TO 8

2½ pounds *tasajo*
  (salt-dried beef)

¼ cup olive oil

2 large onions, sliced

1 green bell pepper, diced

4 garlic cloves, minced

1 cup tomato sauce

1 bay leaf

½ cup *vino seco* (dry white
  cooking wine)

½ teaspoon ground oregano

½ teaspoon ground cumin

½ teaspoon pepper

Arroz Blanco (White Rice)
  (page 82), for serving

Tostones (Fried Green
  Plantains) (page 97),
  for serving

At least 24 hours in advance, cut the *tasajo* in 2 to 3 pieces and place it in a large pot. Add enough cool water to cover and let the beef soak overnight.

Drain the *tasajo*, discard the water, and add more cool water to cover. Bring the water to a boil, then reduce heat to medium-low, cover the pot, and simmer for 1½ to 2 hours. Remove the pot from the heat and let the stock cool completely.

Remove the *tasajo* from the stock, cut it into 2-inch pieces, then shred the pieces. Set aside.

Heat the olive oil in a large frying pan over medium heat. Add the onions, bell pepper and garlic and sauté for 5 to 7 minutes, until the onions are soft and translucent. Add the tomato sauce, bay leaf, *vino seco*, oregano, cumin, and pepper, and cook for 5 minutes. Reduce the heat to low, stir in the shredded beef, and let the soup simmer for 30 to 45 minutes, allowing the flavors to fully develop. Remove and discard the bay leaf.

Serve with *Arroz Blanco* and *Tostones* (Fried Green Plantains).

Arroz con Huevos Fritos

RICE WITH FRIED EGGS

This meal is a childhood favorite. This is the dish most Cuban moms make when their cupboards are barren. It became very popular when Cuban families first immigrated to America, because it is so inexpensive to make and kids just love it! No matter what you have in your cupboards, a steaming bowl of rice topped with fried eggs hits the spot every time.

SERVES 1

¼ cup corn or canola oil

1 cup cooked *Arroz Blanco* (White Rice) (page 82)

2 large eggs

Salt and pepper

Heat the oil in a large frying pan over medium-high heat.

Place the rice in a bowl or mound it on a small plate.

Working with one egg at a time, crack the eggs into a small bowl, pour them into the hot oil, and fry them until they are somewhat firm but still soft in the middle. Carefully spoon some hot oil on top of the egg to cook it slightly, creating a thin white film.

Using a large slotted spoon, remove the eggs from the oil and drain them over a paper towel before placing them on top of the rice. Season with salt and pepper to taste.

Arroz Imperial

CHICKEN AND RICE CASSEROLE

If you've never had Arroz Imperial, *you're in for a treat. Almost everyone has tried* Arroz con Pollo *(Chicken with Rice).* Arroz Imperial *is basically* Arroz con Pollo *in casserole form. It's like a lasagna—layers of rice and chicken are finished off with a layer of cheese and a thin coat of mayonnaise (trust me, it's good). The result is a great make-ahead party dish that only requires a fork and a hearty appetite to enjoy it.*

SERVES 6 TO 8

¼ cup olive oil

1 large onion, diced

1 medium green bell pepper, diced

3 garlic cloves, minced

1½ cups tomato sauce

¼ cup *vino seco* (dry white cooking wine)

1 bay leaf

1 whole chicken, roasted, bones and skin removed, and chopped

4 cups low-sodium chicken stock

1½ teaspoons *Bijol*

2 cups long-grain white rice

½ cup freshly grated Parmesan cheese

1 cup mayonnaise (I prefer Hellman's)

Salt and pepper

Tostones (Fried Green Plantains) (page 97), for serving

Heat the olive oil in a large saucepan over medium heat. Add the onion, bell pepper, and garlic, and sauté for 5 to 7 minutes, until the onions are translucent. Be careful not to brown the vegetables. Add the tomato sauce, *vino seco*, and bay leaf, and cook for another 5 minutes. Add the chicken, stir well, and cook for 3 minutes. Remove from the heat and set aside. Remove and discard the bay leaf.

Bring the stock to a boil over high heat in a large saucepan. Add the *Bijol* and rice, and bring the mixture to a boil again. Cook, uncovered, for 5 minutes. Reduce the heat to low, fluff the rice with a fork, cover the pan, and cook for 17 to 20 minutes, until the rice is tender and fluffy. Taste the rice and season with salt and pepper to taste.

Preheat the oven to 375°F.

Butter the bottom and sides of a 3-quart rectangular casserole dish. Spread a thin layer of rice, about ¼-inch-thick, in the dish, then add a layer of the chicken mixture. Spread half the remaining rice on top of the chicken, then spread the remaining chicken mixture on top of that. Top the layers with the remaining rice.

Combine the Parmesan cheese with the mayonnaise and spread it evenly across the top of the casserole.

Bake the casserole for 10 to 15 minutes, until the top of the casserole is lightly browned. Serve with *Tostones* (Fried Green Plantains).

Arroz con Pollo

CHICKEN WITH RICE

After black beans, this is perhaps the most requested dish at any Cuban restaurant. You should know that nothing—and I mean nothing—compares to homemade Arroz con Pollo. *The dry, pale, yellow rice with the equally dismal looking chicken that is served at most restaurants and "food by the pound" places (the horror!) are not what we will be making here. The homemade result is substantially more satisfying. Hmmm . . . substantial and satisfying, what a concept!*

SERVES 6 TO 8

¼ cup olive oil

1 (5- to 7-pound) chicken, cut into 8 pieces, or 4 or 5 large, bone-in skinless chicken breasts

Salt and pepper

3 garlic cloves, minced

1 large onion, chopped

1 medium green bell pepper, chopped

1 (8-ounce) can tomato sauce

2 (5-gram) packets Goya brand *Sazón con Azafrán*

1 bay leaf

1 cup *vino seco* (dry white cooking wine), or 1 (12-ounce) can beer

2 cups Valencia, Arborio, or other short-grain rice

6 cups chicken stock

1 (8.5-ounce) can peas (do not drain)

1 (8.5-ounce) can roasted red peppers, chopped

continued

Heat the olive oil in a large Dutch oven or ovenproof pot over medium to medium-high heat.

Season the chicken generously with salt and pepper, then add it to the pot in batches and sear it, skin side down, for 3 to 5 minutes, until lightly browned. Do not turn it too soon, as it will stick. Be careful not to crowd the pan. (Putting too many pieces of chicken in the pot at once will cause the heat to dissipate, and you'll end up with steamed chicken.) Transfer the chicken to a plate and set aside.

Add the garlic, onion, and bell pepper to the same pot and sauté for about 10 minutes, until soft. Add the tomato sauce and let it simmer for 5 minutes. Add the *Sazón*, bay leaf, and *vino seco*, and cook for 5 more minutes. Add the rice and stir until it is fully incorporated into the tomato mixture. Add 4 cups of stock and the liquid from the canned peas, and stir. Add the chicken and top with as much of the remaining stock as your pot will allow while leaving about 3 inches of space at the top of the pot. Bring to a boil, cover, and reduce the heat to low. Cook for 10 to 15 minutes.

Preheat the oven to 350°F.

Transfer the entire pot, lid and all, to the oven. (If your pot has a plastic handle, wrap it in foil to protect it from the oven's heat.) Bake for 30 to 40 minutes, until the rice is uniformly cooked (once the grain expands). The liquid need not be fully absorbed for

continued

Tostones (Fried Green
  Plantains) (page 97) or
  Mariquitas (Plantain Chips)
  (page 99), for serving

the rice to be ready. You can cook this longer, depending on how soupy (or *a la chorrera*) you like it. Remember that the liquid continues to evaporate with the residual heat, even out of the oven, so take it out when it is a little soupier than you want it to be. Remove and discard the bay leaf.

Decorate the top of the rice with the peas and red peppers, and serve with *Tostones* (Fried Green Plantains) or *Mariquitas* (Plantain Chips).

Pollo Asado
ROAST CHICKEN

This simple dish is a joy to make because it is effortless and fills your home with the undeniable aroma of home cookin'. Everyone loves that.

1½ cups sour orange juice
(from about 6 oranges)
or a mixture of equal parts
lime juice and orange juice,
reserve the squeezed half
of one orange

8 garlic cloves, minced

Salt and pepper

1 (5- to 7-pound)
whole roaster chicken

1 tablespoon sweet paprika

1 teaspoon dried oregano
leaves

4 tablespoons salted butter

2 medium sweet onions,
1 peeled and left whole,
and 1 quartered

1 bay leaf

4 large carrots, peeled, cut in
half lengthwise, then cut in
half again

4 medium red potatoes, peeled
and cut into 2- to 3-inch
pieces

¾ cup dry white wine

¼ cup olive oil

1 cup chicken stock

Combine the orange juice, garlic, and salt and pepper to taste.

Season the chicken generously with paprika, oregano, and salt and pepper. Place the chicken breast-side down in a large bowl. Pour the orange juice marinade over the chicken, cover it tightly with plastic wrap, and refrigerate for at least 8 hours or overnight.

Preheat the oven to 375°F. Coat a large roasting pan with olive oil.

Remove the chicken from the marinade, reserving the marinade, and place it breast side up in the roasting pan. Rub the top and sides of the chicken with 2 tablespoons of the butter. Put the reserved orange half inside the cavity of the chicken, along with the whole onion and the bay leaf. Arrange the quartered onion, carrots, and potatoes around the chicken.

Roast the chicken for 1½ to 2 hours, depending on the size of the chicken (allow 20 minutes per pound). You may cover the pan loosely with foil for the first hour of roasting to prevent the breast from drying out, but remove it during the last hour so the skin browns. Let the chicken rest for 15 minutes before carving.

Bring the marinade to a boil in a large saucepan. Add the wine, olive oil, and stock, and let boil for 10 to 15 minutes, until the marinade reduces by half and thickens. Add the remaining butter at the end to further thicken the sauce. Add salt and pepper if necessary and serve alongside the chicken.

Note: To determine when a roast chicken is completely cooked, prick the leg with a fork. The chicken is ready when the juices run clear.

Pollo Frito
CUBAN-STYLE FRIED CHICKEN

Fried chicken is delicious, any way you slice it. Wait . . . oh right! You don't slice fried chicken. You don't even need a fork or knife to eat it. And isn't that the point really, to have an excuse to eat with your hands? Which is one reason I think this Cuban-style fried chicken makes a great "date" meal. Wait—hear me out! First, when you make Pollo Frito, *your entire house—make that your entire neighborhood—will smell like Eau de Cuban House. This, of course, will impress everybody, including your date. Second, and perhaps best of all, you can eat with your hands. Finally—and here's the clincher—you can lick your fingers! Now, what better way to appeal to the opposite sex? Anyway, if you're on a date or not, please don't be one of those people who insist on eating this meal with utensils. Please!*

This recipe requires you to cut a whole fryer chicken into eight pieces. If you are like me—averse to wrestling with uncooked chicken—have your butcher cut it up for you. It's much faster, and less messy.

SERVES 6

- 1 cup sour orange juice (from about 4 oranges), or equal parts lime and orange juice
- 6 garlic cloves, minced
- 1 tablespoon plus 2 teaspoons salt
- 1 teaspoon pepper
- 1 (5- to 7-pound) whole fryer chicken, cut into 8 pieces
- 4 cups corn oil
- 2 cups all-purpose flour
- 1 tablespoon paprika
- ½ teaspoon dried oregano leaves
- 1 teaspoon onion powder
- 4 large eggs, beaten

Combine the orange juice, garlic, 1 tablespoon of the salt, and ½ teaspoon of the pepper in a large bowl.

Arrange the chicken in a large glass baking pan, pour the orange juice mixture over it, cover with plastic wrap, and refrigerate for at least 8 hours, preferably overnight. Turn the chicken once during the marinating process.

Heat the oil to about 375°F in a large, deep cast iron skillet over medium-high heat.

Remove the chicken from the marinade and discard the marinade.

Combine the flour, 2 teaspoons of the salt, ½ teaspoon of the pepper, the paprika, oregano, and onion powder in a large bowl and mix well. Dredge each piece of chicken lightly in the flour, then in the beaten eggs, and again in the flour, making sure the chicken is completely coated.

Add four pieces of chicken to the oil and fry them on one side for 8 to 10 minutes, until they turn medium brown on the cooking side. If the chicken is browning too rapidly, reduce the heat slightly.

continued

Turn the chicken over and cook for 4 to 5 minutes. Transfer the chicken to drain on a wire rack placed over paper towels or brown paper bags. Bring the oil back up to 375°F and fry the remaining pieces of chicken in the same manner. Let the chicken cool slightly before serving (this also enhances the crispiness of the chicken).

Note: Remember to let the oil return to the desired temperature before frying the second batch of chicken. This will ensure that the chicken does not absorb excess oil.

Pollo Empanizado
BREADED FRIED CHICKEN

I love to make this recipe for kids. I always cut the chicken into small, bite-sized pieces, like chicken fingers. I get a kick out of watching them plan on dipping the chicken in some sort of sauce, but once they take the first bite of the chicken, the sauce is history!

SERVES 4

4 garlic cloves, minced

¼ cup sour orange juice, or a mixture of equal parts lime juice and orange juice

4 boneless and skinless chicken breasts, cut into strips or pounded to ¼-inch-thickness

½ cup olive oil

¼ cup all-purpose flour

¾ cup finely ground cracker meal

4 eggs

½ teaspoon paprika

Salt and pepper

Lime wedges, for serving

Combine the garlic and orange juice in a glass or ceramic dish, and add the chicken. Toss to completely coat the chicken with the marinade, cover with plastic wrap, and let the chicken marinate at room temperature for at least 1 hour.

Heat the olive oil in a large frying pan over medium-high heat. Combine the flour with the cracker meal in a shallow plate and set aside. Beat the eggs, add the paprika, and beat again to combine.

Remove the chicken from the marinade and pat it dry. Season it liberally with salt and pepper, dip it in the egg, then in the flour mixture. Dip the chicken a second time in the egg, then the flour mixture. Shake off any excess and gently lay the chicken in the hot oil. Fry for 4 to 5 minutes on each side, until golden brown. Transfer the chicken to a paper towel–lined platter.

Serve with a squeeze of lime.

Fricase de Pollo

CHICKEN FRICASSEE

This dish is another of the many tomato-based, one-dish wonders that Cubans enjoy. This is also great the day after it's cooked, making for fantastic leftovers. While the traditional recipe calls for a whole chicken, cut up, my family prefers white meat, so I make this with six large, bone-in chicken breasts. You can do either.

SERVES 6

½ cup olive oil

6 large chicken breasts, bone-in, or 1 (5- to 7-pound) whole fryer chicken, cut into 8 pieces

1 tablespoon salt

1 teaspoon pepper

4 garlic cloves, minced

1 large onion, chopped

1 medium green bell pepper, chopped

2 cups tomato sauce

1 cup chicken stock

½ cup *vino seco* (dry white cooking wine)

1 bay leaf

1 teaspoon dried oregano leaves

½ teaspoon cumin

1 teaspoon sweet paprika

4 medium red potatoes, peeled and cut into 2- to 3-inch pieces

½ cup pimento-stuffed olives

Arroz Blanco (White Rice) (page 82), for serving

Platanitos Maduros (Fried Sweet Plantains) (page 94), for serving

Heat half of the olive oil in a large heavy pot over medium-high heat.

Season the chicken with the salt and pepper, then add it to the pot and sear it for 4 to 5 minutes, turning once, until the outside of the chicken pieces turns light golden brown. Transfer the chicken to a plate and set aside.

Heat the remaining olive oil in the pot. Add the garlic, onion, and pepper, and sauté for 10 to 12 minutes, until the onion slightly caramelizes. Add the tomato sauce, stock, *vino seco*, bay leaf, oregano, cumin, and paprika, and bring to a boil. Add the chicken and potatoes and reduce the heat to low. Cover the pot and cook for 1 hour.

Add the olives and stir well. Taste and adjust the seasonings, if necessary. Remove and discard the bay leaf.

Serve with white rice and *Platanitos Maduros* (Fried Sweet Plantains).

Bistec de Pollo a la Plancha

GRILLED CHICKEN BREAST

I tell you, finding a low-calorie recipe in this book is like searching for Sasquatch or the Loch Ness Monster. But what could be more healthful than a grilled chicken breast? This one is full of flavor because of the sour orange marinade. So whenever you feel you've overindulged by eating every other recipe in this book, why not make Bistec de Pollo a la Plancha *with a salad? You'll need to skip the rice and beans, of course.*

SERVES 4

4 garlic cloves, minced

½ teaspoon paprika

½ cup sour orange juice, or a mixture of equal parts lime juice and orange juice

4 boneless, skinless chicken breasts, pounded to ¼-inch-thickness

¼ cup olive oil

Salt and pepper

1 medium onion, thinly sliced

Lime wedges

Combine the garlic, paprika, and orange juice in a nonreactive dish, then add the chicken and move it around so it is completely coated with the marinade. Cover the dish with plastic wrap and let the chicken marinate at room temperature for at least 1 hour.

Heat the olive oil in a large frying pan over medium-high heat.

Remove the chicken from the marinade (*do not discard the marinade*), pat it dry, and season it liberally with salt and pepper. Add the chicken to the hot oil and sear it for 4 to 5 minutes on each side, until golden brown. Transfer the chicken to a serving dish and cover it with foil to keep it warm.

In the same pan, add the onion and sauté for 3 minutes over medium-high heat, stirring frequently to prevent the onion from burning. Add the reserved marinade and bring the mixture to a boil; let it boil for 5 to 7 minutes. Pour the onion mixture over the chicken breasts and serve immediately with lime wedges.

Pavo de Thanksgiving con Relleno de Jamón
THANKSGIVING DAY TURKEY WITH HAM STUFFING

Most Cubans don't celebrate Thanksgiving in Cuba, but here en el exilio (in exile), we have taken on the culinary tradition and made it our own. We call it Sansgivin (Thanksgiving in broken English), and we feel very American partaking in this holiday. I suspect many Cubans do not really understand the whole pilgrim-and-Indian concept, although some will feign vast knowledge about the first Thanksgiving. I have witnessed grandfathers giving long—partially accurate, partially fabricated, and very humorous—dissertations to their grandchildren about Sansgivin. When the story starts with a pilgrim named Pepe, you know you're in trouble.

Turkey, or el pavo, is a once-a-year thing for Cubans, and how it is prepared is open to interpretation. Each family handles the turkey in their own special way. For example, some insist on being true to tradition and try to make an "Americanized" bird. This is always a disaster. You see, Cubans generally don't cook with spices like sage and rosemary, so when they use them . . . well, we overuse them! The turkey ends up tasting a little like perfume! Then there are those who get upset when the turkey actually ends up tasting like turkey, despite the fact that they desperately attempted to make it taste like roast pork!

Then there is the Cuban take on what should be served alongside the bird on Thanksgiving. There may be some mashed potatoes (there is documented evidence of mashed potato sightings in East Hialeah), but nine times out of ten, there is una pierna (a leg of pork). You see, Cubans can't live without pork. It's not enough that we always roast an entire pig on Christmas Eve. We need pork at Thanksgiving, as well. As a matter of fact, even our stuffing is made with pork—and I've given you a recipe for that here. This is no Stove Top Stuffing, but rather a meal in itself. It has flavors of nutmeg, garlic, and sherry and is studded with raisins and slivered almonds. I like to lightly roast the almonds in the toaster oven at 300°F for five minutes before adding them to the stuffing. The crunchiness adds a nice texture to the dish. After tasting this stuffing, you'll wonder why you made the turkey—although, after tasting the turkey, you'll be glad you did.

SERVES 8 TO 10

Turkey

14- to 16-pound turkey
Salt and pepper
½ cup olive oil
2½ to 3 cups orange juice
1 cup chicken stock

continued

To make the turkey, season it generously with salt and pepper, including the inside of the cavity. Place the turkey, breast-side down, inside a container large enough to accommodate it overnight in the refrigerator. You may use a roasting pan if it is nonreactive and deep enough to hold the marinade.

Combine the oil, orange juice, stock, garlic, onion, paprika, oregano, and cumin in a large bowl. Carefully pour the marinade over the turkey, cover it with plastic wrap, and refrigerate it overnight.

continued

12 garlic cloves, minced

1 large onion, diced

1 tablespoon sweet paprika

1 teaspoon dried oregano
     leaves

1 teaspoon ground cumin

¼ pound (1 stick) butter

Stuffing

¼ pound (1 stick) butter, plus
     more as needed

1 large onion, chopped

3 garlic cloves, minced

1½ pounds ground sweet or
     honey-baked ham

8 ounces cream cheese,
     softened

½ cup *vino seco*
     (dry white cooking wine)

1 loaf day-old Cuban or French
     bread, cut into bite-sized
     pieces

1 teaspoon ground nutmeg

1 teaspoon salt

½ cup low-sodium chicken stock

½ teaspoon white pepper

1 cup heavy cream

¾ cup slivered almonds

¾ cup raisins

The next morning (at least 10 hours before serving), remove the turkey and the stick of butter from the refrigerator and let them come to room temperature.

Meanwhile, prepare the stuffing. Preheat the oven to 350°F. Butter a large rectangular casserole dish.

Melt the butter in a large pot over medium heat. Add the onion and garlic, and sauté for 5 to 7 minutes, until the onion softens. Add the ham, cream cheese, and *vino seco*, and cook for 10 minutes, stirring frequently until the ingredients are fully incorporated. Set aside.

Place the bread pieces in a large bowl. Combine the nutmeg, salt, pepper, stock and cream in a small bowl, and pour the mixture over the bread. Toss to combine. Add the almonds and raisins and toss again. Add the ham mixture and mix well. Pour the bread mixture into the prepared casserole dish, cover it with foil, and bake for 1 hour, removing the foil after 30 minutes. Let the stuffing cool to room temperature.

Preheat the oven to 400°F.

Remove the turkey from the marinade (discard the marinade), and place it in a roasting pan. Rub the butter over the entire turkey, massaging it well. Use your fingers to gently separate the skin from the meat around the breast bone, and rub some butter into the flesh, as well. Stuff the cavity of the turkey with the stuffing.

Roast the turkey for 10 minutes. Reduce the oven temperature to 325°F, loosely cover the bird with foil, and roast for 4 hours. Remove the foil and continue roasting, basting every half hour or so, for 2 to 5 additional hours, depending on the size of your turkey. The turkey and stuffing will both be cooked when they reach 165°F when tested with a cooking thermometer.

Let the turkey rest for 20 to 25 minutes before carving.

Note: To make a quick gravy, combine the pan drippings with 2 tablespoons of butter in a saucepan and bring to a boil. Add 2 cups low-sodium chicken stock and boil for 5 minutes. Drain through a fine sieve if the dark bits in the pan drippings bother you. Place ¼ cup of the gravy in a small bowl, add 1½ tablespoons all-purpose flour, and mix well. Slowly add the flour mixture to the gravy, whisking consistently until no lumps are visible. Bring the gravy to a boil and stir until the gravy is thickened. Serve warm.

Escabeche
PICKLED SWORDFISH

If you always have friends dropping by for drinks and hors d'oeuvres, escabeche *is a great treat to have around. It is a little labor intensive, but it stays fresh a long, long time—the fish will keep in its marinade, covered tightly, for up to one month. And you don't even need to refrigerate it. Oh, and it's good for you, too.*

SERVES 6

3 to 4 cups cup olive oil, plus more as needed

3 pounds (1-inch-thick) swordfish steaks

1 cup all-purpose flour

2 large onions, sliced

1 large green bell pepper, sliced

1 large red bell pepper, sliced

3 cups white vinegar, plus more as needed

1 cup pimento-stuffed olives

½ cup large capers

1 tablespoon salt

1 teaspoon pepper

1 teaspoon paprika

Pan de Ajo (Cuban Garlic Bread) (page 97) or saltines, for serving

Heat 1 cup of the olive oil in a large frying pan over medium heat. Dredge the fish steaks in the flour, then add them to the hot oil and fry them for 3 minutes on each side, until golden. Place the fish in a single layer in a large glass or terracotta container that has a lid. Set aside to cool.

In the same oil in which the fish was fried, gently sauté the onions and peppers, in several batches if necessary. Transfer them to the container with the fish, layering them atop the fish.

Combine the remaining olive oil and the white vinegar in a large bowl and stir in the olives, capers, salt, pepper, and paprika. Pour this mixture evenly over the fish and peppers. Cover the container tightly and set aside to marinate, at room temperature, for 7 days, turning the fish every day or two.

After 7 days, taste the marinade and adjust the seasonings, if necessary.

Serve with *Pan de Ajo* (Cuban Garlic Bread) or saltines.

Huevos a la Malagueña
MÁLAGA-STYLE EGGS

People rarely think of eggs as a dinner dish, but they really are a great high-protein option. Huevos a la Malagueña *originated in Spain and are similar to French coddled eggs. The eggs are served on top of savory sofrito, which provides an unexpected burst of flavor. The addition of ham and shrimp complete the meal with lots of added protein. This dish is as elegant as it is delicious. It also makes a great brunch dish. Follow it up with My Big Fat Cuban Torrejas (page 204) for dessert.*

SERVES 6

18 small shrimp

¼ cup olive oil

1 medium onion, chopped

2 garlic cloves, minced

1 small green bell pepper, chopped

2 cups tomato sauce

1 bay leaf

1 teaspoon salt, plus more as needed

½ teaspoon pepper, plus more as needed

½ teaspoon paprika

½ cup *vino seco* (dry white cooking wine)

12 large eggs

6 tablespoons butter, melted

½ pound Serrano ham, cut into thin strips

1 cup canned asparagus tips

½ cup canned peas

2 tablespoons chopped fresh parsley

Preheat the oven to 350°F.

Bring 3 cups of lightly salted water to a boil in a large pan. Add the shrimp and boil for 2 to 3 minutes, until the shrimp are opaque. Drain the shrimp and set them aside to cool. Peel and devein the shrimp.

Heat the olive oil in a medium-sized frying pan over medium heat. Add the onion, garlic, and bell pepper, and sauté for 5 to 7 minutes, until the vegetables are soft. Add the tomato sauce, bay leaf, salt, pepper, paprika, and *vino seco*. Reduce the heat to low, cover the pan, and let the sauce simmer for 10 to 15 minutes, until the sauce thickens slightly. Remove and discard the bay leaf. Divide the mixture evenly among six 6-ounce ramekins.

Place about ¼ cup of the mixture into each of six 6-ounce ramekins. Layer each dish evenly with ham, shrimp, asparagus, and peas. Divide the remaining tomato mixture evenly among the ramekins. Carefully break 2 eggs into each ramekin and drizzle with 1 tablespoon melted butter.

Place the ramekins on a baking sheet and bake for 12 to 14 minutes, until the egg whites are set (completely white). Sprinkle with parsley and salt and pepper to taste.

Arroz con Camarones
SHRIMP AND RICE

I love this dish because I always really disliked paella—it is such a mish mash of fish, shellfish, chicken, sausage, clams, and mussels. You never know what you're going to get, and as a child, I really hated that. I've learned to appreciate good paella now, but there is something so comforting about digging into a pot of saffron-infused rice and knowing that it is full of plump, juicy, delicious shrimp, and no other surprises.

For the shrimp stock in this recipe, you can use the store-bought kind or make your own by boiling washed shrimp carcasses (after peeling) in equal parts chicken stock and water. When this dish is done cooking, all of the stock will not be absorbed by the rice. But don't worry, it's meant to be kind of soupy. It will dry out a little as it sits on your plate.

SERVES 6 TO 8

½ cup olive oil

1½ pounds large shrimp, peeled and deveined

3 garlic cloves, minced

1 green bell pepper, chopped

1 large onion, chopped

1 cup tomato sauce

1 bay leaf

½ cup *vino seco* (dry white cooking wine)

1 tablespoon red wine vinegar

½ teaspoon ground oregano

½ teaspoon ground cumin

1½ teaspoons *Bijol*

1½ teaspoons salt, plus more as needed

½ teaspoon pepper, plus more as needed

4 cups shrimp or vegetable stock

2 cups short-grain rice

½ cup canned peas, for garnish

½ cup diced pimentos, for garnish

Heat the olive oil in a large pot or Dutch oven over medium-high heat. Add the shrimp and sauté until opaque, 3 to 4 minutes. Set aside.

In the same pot, sauté the garlic, bell pepper, and onion for 5 to 7 minutes, until the onion is translucent. Add the tomato sauce, bay leaf, *vino seco*, vinegar, oregano, cumin, *Bijol*, salt, pepper, and stock, and bring to a boil. Add the rice and cook, uncovered, for 5 minutes. Reduce the heat to low, cover the pot, and cook for 17 to 20 minutes, until the rice becomes tender. Stir in the shrimp. Taste and adjust the seasoning, if necessary. Remove and discard the bay leaf. Garnish with peas and pimentos.

Camarones Enchilados

SHRIMP CREOLE

This shrimp dish is quite typical of Cuban cookery, because the shrimp is slowly simmered in the sofrito, *the tomato-based seasoning that is used to prepare many Cuban dishes. Because shrimp are so delicately flavored, the sauce really penetrates them in this dish, both in flavor and color, making it as vibrant as it is delectable.*

SERVES 6

⅓ cup olive oil

4 garlic cloves, minced

1 large onion, diced

1 medium green bell pepper, diced

1½ cups tomato sauce

½ cup *vino seco* (dry white cooking wine)

½ cup fish or vegetable stock

1 bay leaf

1 teaspoon salt

1 teaspoon pepper

1 teaspoon paprika

½ teaspoon dried oregano leaves

2 pounds medium shrimp, peeled and deveined

Heat the olive oil in a large, heavy pot over medium-high heat. Add the garlic, onion, and bell pepper, and sauté for 5 to 10 minutes, until the vegetables are soft. Add the tomato sauce, *vino seco*, stock, bay leaf, salt, pepper, paprika, and oregano, and bring to a boil. Cover the pot, reduce the heat to low, and simmer for 30 to 40 minutes. Taste the sauce and adjust the seasonings, if necessary.

Raise the heat and bring the sauce to a boil again. Add the shrimp and cook, stirring frequently, for 5 to 10 minutes, until they turn pink. Watch them carefully—it is important not to overcook the shrimp, as this really toughens them. Remove the pot from the heat and let the shrimp sit for a few minutes in the sauce to allow the flavors to fully penetrate them. Remove and discard the bay leaf.

Langosta Enchilada (Lobster Creole): This dish is prepared in exactly the same manner as *Camarones Enchilados*. The only difference is that 6 or 7 medium fresh lobster tails are substituted for the shrimp. To prepare them, cut the tails (shell on), width-wise, into 2- to 3-inch pieces. Add the lobsters to the sauce (with the shell still attached) when the recipe directs you to add the shrimp, and simmer for 15 to 20 minutes, until the meat is completely opaque. Like shrimp, lobster becomes tough and rubbery when it is overcooked, so watch it carefully!

Colas de Langosta a la Crema
LOBSTER IN CREAM SAUCE

This dish is unlike anything else you've encountered in this book so far. It is creamy and decadent and oh so rich—quite different from the savory, tomato-based dishes that abound in this cookbook. It is definitely worth a try. I love making this for dinner parties because it is such an elegant dish. Also, it can be made ahead of time and baked right before serving, making it perfect for entertaining.

SERVES 6

6 tablespoons butter, melted

3 pounds lobster meat, coarsely chopped into ½- to ¾-inch pieces (about 3 cups)

1 tablespoon lemon juice

3 tablespoons *vino seco* (dry white cooking wine)

1 cup whole milk

1 cup half-and-half

½ cup all-purpose flour

4 egg yolks

1 tablespoon Worcestershire sauce

½ teaspoon ground nutmeg

½ teaspoon paprika

1 teaspoon salt

½ teaspoon white pepper

½ cup breadcrumbs

½ cup grated Parmesan cheese

Pan de Ajo (Cuban Garlic Bread) (page 79)

Heat 2 tablespoons of the butter in a large frying pan over medium-high heat. Add the lobster meat, lemon juice, and *vino seco*, and sauté until the lobster is opaque, about 5 minutes. Set aside.

Combine 3 tablespoons of the butter, the milk, half-and-half, flour, egg yolks, Worcestershire sauce, nutmeg, paprika, salt, and pepper in a blender or food processor, and blend until just fully combined. Do not overblend. Pour the mixture into a large saucepan and cook over medium-low heat, whisking continuously, until the sauce thickens and boils. Reduce the heat to low.

Add the lobster to the pan and stir well so the meat is completely incorporated into the sauce. Taste and adjust the seasonings, if necessary.

Preheat the broiler. Lightly butter a 2-quart casserole or gratin dish or spray it with nonstick cooking spray.

Combine the breadcrumbs and Parmesan cheese with the remaining tablespoon of butter in a small bowl and mix well.

Pour the lobster mixture into the prepared dish and sprinkle the top with the breadcrumb mixture. Place the casserole under the broiler for 3 to 5 minutes, until the breadcrumbs turn golden brown.

Serve with *Pan de Ajo* (Cuban Garlic Bread).

Note: Never leave anything in the broiler unattended—it can burn in no time, flat!

Camarones al Ajillo

SHRIMP IN GARLIC SAUCE

This dish was definitely my dad's favorite. He never tired of eating it. Many years ago, on our first trip to Spain, I eagerly ordered the Gambas al Ajillo, *as they refer to this dish there. I was horrified when the waiter brought a small, sizzling clay pot overflowing with humongous, unpeeled shrimp, heads still intact. I was sixteen years old at the time and, frankly, could not bear to look at them. In recent years (ok, maybe not so recent), I have begun to accept that leaving both the shells and heads on shrimp makes this dish more authentic and enhances the flavor. But I say, to heck with authenticity. I like my shrimp peeled, deveined, and not the size of a Buick!*

SERVES 6 TO 8

4 tablespoons salted butter

2 pounds medium shrimp, peeled and deveined, tails on

½ cup olive oil

1 small yellow onion, diced

15 garlic cloves, minced

1 cup shrimp, fish, or vegetable stock, plus more as needed

½ cup dry white wine

Juice of 1 lime

2 teaspoons salt

½ teaspoon white pepper

1 teaspoon all-purpose flour

¼ cup diced parsley

Arroz Blanco (White Rice) (page 82) or *Arroz Amarillo* (Yellow Rice) (page 84), for serving

In a heavy pot, heat 2 tablespoons of the butter over medium heat. Once the butter begins to turn golden brown, add half of the shrimp and quickly sear them (you may have to raise the heat). Transfer the shrimp to a plate and repeat with the remaining butter and shrimp.

In the same pot, heat the olive oil over medium heat. Add the onion and garlic and sauté for 5 to 7 minutes, until both are soft. Add the stock, wine, lime juice, salt, and pepper, and bring to a boil. Reduce the heat to low, cover the pot, and cook for 15 to 20 minutes. You may need to add extra stock if the sauce evaporated too quickly, but not more than ¼ cup.

Measure out ½ cup of the hot liquid and place it in a medium-sized bowl. Add the flour and whisk until smooth. Add the flour mixture to the pot and stir until the sauce thickens to the consistency of light syrup. Add the shrimp and the parsley and stir, incorporating all the ingredients completely. Cook for 5 to 7 minutes. Do not overcook the shrimp, or they will be tough.

Serve with white or saffron-seasoned yellow rice.

Pescado en Salsa Verde

FISH IN PARSLEY AND GARLIC SAUCE

This is a great dish to serve at dinner parties. You can even make it ahead of time and just warm it up when your guests arrive. There are many variations to the preparation of this dish. Some recipes call for combining the raw fish fillets with the garlic parsley sauce and then baking it. Other recipes instruct you to cook the fish first, then pour the sauce over it right before serving. My recipe calls for lightly floured and seared fillets that are then baked in the parsley sauce. It's a little more work, but it's well worth it. The light golden color and flavor the searing imparts on the fish makes a huge difference. I also recommend hand chopping the parsley instead of using a food processor, so it will retain its vibrant green color.

SERVES 6

6 (6- to 8-ounce) red snapper fillets, or other firm-fleshed white fish

2½ teaspoons salt

1 teaspoon white pepper

Juice of 2 limes

½ cup olive oil, plus more as needed

¼ cup all-purpose flour

½ teaspoon paprika

1½ cups chopped parsley

½ cup diced sweet onion (like Vidalia)

3 tablespoons red wine vinegar

½ teaspoon sugar

2 tablespoons salted butter

8 garlic cloves, minced

1 cup dry white wine

Season the fish with 1 teaspoon of salt and ½ teaspoon of pepper, and let it marinate in the lime juice in a nonreactive dish for 30 minutes.

Heat half the olive oil in a large sauté pan over medium-high heat. Combine the flour, ½ teaspoon of the salt, and ½ teaspoon of the white pepper in a shallow platter. Season the fish with 1 teaspoon of the salt and the paprika. Dredge both sides of each fillet lightly in the seasoned flour, add them to the pan, and sear for 2 minutes per side. Remove the fish from the pan and set it aside.

Preheat the oven to 425°F.

In a large bowl, combine the parsley, onion, vinegar, sugar, and the remaining olive oil, white pepper, and salt.

Set the same pan used to sear the fish over medium heat, add the butter and garlic, and lightly sauté for 3 minutes. Add the wine, raise the heat, and bring the mixture to a boil. Allow it to boil for 5 minutes, then reduce the heat to low, add the parsley mixture, and stir well. Cook for 5 minutes.

Lightly coat the bottom of a shallow, nonreactive baking dish with olive oil. Arrange the fillets in the dish so they do not overlap.

Taste the parsley sauce and add salt, if necessary. Pour the sauce over the fish and bake for 5 minutes. Reduce the oven temperature to 375°F and continue baking for an additional 15 to 20 minutes, until the fish is thoroughly cooked. Remove the fish from the oven and let it sit for 5 to 10 minutes before serving.

Bacalao a la Vizcaina

COD IN SPICY TOMATO SAUCE

My mom used to make this dish every year on Good Friday, the Friday preceding Easter Sunday. It is one of those childhood traditions I remember fondly. Most Cubans have their own interpretation of this unique and tasty dish that originated in Spain. The flavor of this dish is wonderful—the tanginess of the tomato sauce coupled with the delicate fish is a delectable combination.

Get started on this recipe at least a day in advance, because you'll have to soak your salt cod for at least twelve hours before cooking it. This recipe works best with day-old Cuban bread.

SERVES 6

1½ pounds salt cod

1 cup olive oil

½ cup all-purpose flour

5 garlic cloves, minced

2 large onions, chopped

1 large green bell pepper, chopped

3 cups tomato sauce

½ cup *vino seco* (dry white cooking wine)

2 bay leaves

1 tablespoon sweet paprika

1 teaspoon salt

½ teaspoon white pepper

4 medium to large red potatoes, cut into 2-inch cubes

1 (2-foot) loaf Cuban bread or French bread

6 hard-boiled eggs, sliced lengthwise, for garnish

½ cup pimentos, for garnish

½ cup peas, for garnish

1 tablespoon Tabasco sauce, for garnish

Arroz Blanco (White Rice) (page 82), for serving

Place the cod in a large bowl and add cool water to cover. Let the cod soak at room temperature for 10 to 12 hours, changing the water every 1 to 2 hours.

Drain the cod and put it in a large pot. Fill the pot three-quarters full with water and bring to a boil. Boil uncovered for 5 to 10 minutes, then reduce the heat to low, cover the pot, and cook for 10 minutes. Reserve 2 cups of the cod cooking water, then drain the cod, discarding the remaining water. Set the cod aside to cool completely.

Heat ¼ cup of the olive oil in a large frying pan over medium-high heat. Cut the cod into large (2- to 3-inch) chunks; remove any bones. Lightly dredge the pieces in the flour and shake off any excess. Carefully place the fish in the hot oil and fry it for 2 to 3 minutes per side, until it turns a light golden color. Transfer the fish to a paper towel–lined plate and set aside.

In the same pot used to boil the cod, heat ½ cup of the olive oil over medium heat. Add the garlic, onions, and bell pepper, and sauté for 10 to 12 minutes, until the vegetables soften and the onion and garlic attain a light golden hue. Add the tomato sauce, *vino seco*, bay leaves, paprika, salt, and pepper. Raise the heat to high and bring the mixture to a boil, stirring frequently. Let the mixture boil for 3 to 5 minutes, reduce the heat to low, add the potatoes and the reserved cooking liquid, and cover. Cook for 25 to 30 minutes, until the potatoes are fork-tender. Add the cod and stir,

continued

incorporating it completely into the sauce.

In the pan used to fry the cod, heat the remaining ¼ cup olive oil over medium-high heat. Cut the bread into 1½- to 2-inch-thick slices and add to the hot oil. Carefully fry the bread for about 1 minute on each side, until golden brown. Sprinkle lightly with salt, if desired.

To serve, spoon the fish stew onto a plate and garnish with hard-boiled eggs, pimentos, peas, and Tabasco sauce. Serve with hot, fluffy, white rice and the fried bread.

Pargo Frito

FRIED SNAPPER

I love this dish; it is so simple to make. But don't eat this when you are starving, or you will end up having to dislodge fish bones from your throat! (Not fun.) This is a meal that is meant to be savored slowly. White rice, black beans, and Tostones *(Fried Green Plantains) or* Platanitos Maduros *(Fried Sweet Plantains) (pages 97 and 94) are the perfect side dishes, and be sure to have lots of fresh lime and hot sauce on hand. A cold beer wouldn't hurt either.*

I prefer frying this outdoors whenever possible. Remember to always start with the freshest fish you can find—one that smells like the ocean and has clear eyes. It should not smell overwhelmingly fishy.

SERVES 4

½ cup sour orange juice, or a mixture of equal parts lime juice and orange juice

6 garlic cloves, minced

3 tablespoons olive oil

½ teaspoon paprika

¼ teaspoon ground cumin

½ teaspoon salt, plus more as needed

3 to 4 cups canola oil

Pepper

1 cup all-purpose flour

4 (1-pound each) whole red snappers, scaled, gutted, and cleaned, head left intact

Hot sauce, optional

Combine the sour orange juice, garlic, olive oil, paprika, cumin, and salt in a small saucepan over medium-high heat and cook for 7 to 10 minutes, stirring frequently until the sauce thickens slightly. Set aside.

Heat the oil—making sure there is enough for the fish to be at least halfway submerged—in a deep fryer or large, deep frying pan over medium-high heat.

Season the fish with salt and pepper and dredge them in flour. Fry each fish separately, turning once after 4 to 5 minutes. The fish will be ready in 8 to 10 minutes. Transfer the fish to a paper towel–lined plate and continue with the remaining fish.

Place the fried fish on a serving platter, top with the sour orange sauce, and season with hot sauce.

Postres

DESSERTS

I am going to make a very broad statement here.

Ready? Here goes . . . no self-respecting Cuban can leave the dinner table without dessert.

I personally consider the rest of the meal as a kind of foreplay, if you will. All those distractions: setting the table, preparing the appetizers, the main course, the side dishes, the salad . . . it's all just a farce. A cruel and sinister conspiracy to keep me from the ecstasy that is DESSERRRRTTTT!!!!!!!!!!!!!!

Sorry, I get a little carried away. Just for your general information, by dessert I mean anything containing a respectable amount of sugar. A one-pound bag of pure cane sugar would qualify. Truth be told, I am sort of a dessert junkie. Maybe you noticed? I need my fix regularly. Oh I've tried "rehab"—Equal, Splenda, Sweet 'n Low, duct tape, nothing worked! Most Cubans have the same love-hate relationship with sugar. I suspect it's genetic. I, for one, blame my mother for this addiction. Back in the day, the fatter the baby, the more beautiful she was. Well, let me tell you, I was gorgeous! Looking back at my baby pictures, I realize how difficult it must have been for me to develop motor skills since I didn't seem to have any wrists. I am not kidding—my upper extremities went from fat arm to fat hand. No evidence of a wrist anywhere.

Cubans eat dessert, period. Something about our food almost requires it. It does not have to be a giant piece of flan. A little sliver of anything sweet will do. I think that is why guava paste and cream cheese or even canned papaya chunks are so popular in Cuban households. They are easy to always have on hand. If you really want to treat yourself or are planning a gathering of any kind, you must make two or preferably three of the recipes in this section. Followed by a shot of Cuban coffee, of course!

Dulce de Leche
CARAMEL SAUCE

This is the only one-ingredient recipe you will find in this book, yet as I write this, my mouth waters. Nothing, and I mean, nothing, compares to the caramely goodness of dulce de leche. *Some people may think—and they are mistaken—that Häagen-Dazs invented this delectable golden delicacy. Cubans have been making* dulce de leche *for decades. Why not make some yourself? It's easy and delicious on everything—especially right out of the can!*

Dulce de leche, *which translates roughly as "candy of milk," is not hard to make, it just takes a bit of time and attention. There are several ways to make it—I provide you with three. Now you have no excuse not to make this!*

MAKES ABOUT 1½ CUPS

1 (14-ounce) can sweetened condensed milk

My preferred method for making *dulce de leche* is the classic in-the-can method. It's quite simple: Place the unopened can of sweetened condensed milk in a large saucepan, add enough water to completely submerge the can, then bring the water to a boil. Lower the heat slightly and keep the water at a low boil for 2 to 3 hours, making sure the water level always stays above the top of the can. *This is very important! If the can is not submerged at all times, it could explode.* The longer it cooks, the thicker and darker the *dulce de leche* will be; after 2 hours, you'll be able to drizzle it; after 3 hours, it will be thick enough to sandwich between cookies. Let the can cool thoroughly before you open it.

Another way of making *dulce de leche* is with a pressure cooker. Although this method is much faster than the method above, the idea of putting a sealed can that is under pressure inside a pressure cooker that is under pressure is not my cup of tea! But try it if you're brave: Place the can in the pressure cooker and submerge it completely in water. Follow the manufacturer's directions to cook it for 20 to 30 minutes.

The fastest and safest method to make *dulce de leche* is to pour the condensed milk into a small saucepan and simmer it over low heat, stirring constantly, until the milk achieves the consistency and color you desire.

Natilla

VANILLA CUSTARD

Natilla *is basically Cuban* crème brûlée *or a rich vanilla pudding. Most places serve traditional* natilla *with a light sprinkling of cinnamon. However, you can take out your handy dandy kitchen torch, caramelize some sugar on top, and call it* Crema a la Catalana. *No matter what you call it, this dessert is creamy, dense, delicious, and fattening! Now, how many things can you say that about? Ok, don't answer that.*

Don't you dare use low-fat milk in this recipe. It will affect both the taste and the consistency. So just splurge. As for the vanilla, my mom insists white vanilla is better, so if you can find it, use it.

SERVES 8

1 cup condensed milk
3 cups whole milk
8 large egg yolks
¾ cup sugar
¼ teaspoon salt
¼ cup cornstarch
2 teaspoons pure vanilla extract
Ground cinnamon, for sprinkling

Combine the milks, egg yolks, sugar, salt, and cornstarch in a large bowl. Stir or whisk well, until the sugar is completely dissolved. Strain the mixture through a fine sieve into a heavy saucepan. Stir in the vanilla and set the pan over medium heat. Cook the mixture, stirring continuously with a whisk or wooden spoon, until it begins to boil. (My mother insists you use a wooden spoon, and stir the *natilla* using a figure-eight motion. She insists on a lot of things! My friend's mom insists that the spoon must make this noise—"taka taka taka"—when it hits the sides of the saucepan. . . . Yeah, don't ask!) Reduce the heat to medium-low and cook until the custard thickens, for 15 to 20 minutes.

Pour the custard into individual ramekins and set aside to cool to room temperature. Cover the ramekins lightly with plastic wrap, and refrigerate for at least 1 hour, until the custard sets. Sprinkle with cinnamon immediately before serving.

Tita's Panetela

MY MOM'S FAMOUS BUTTER POUND CAKE

My daughters have always called my mother Tita, which, I suppose, is short for abuelita *("grandmother" in Spanish). My mother's pound cake is the best, hands down! It was the base for all of my elaborate childhood birthday cakes, but it is probably best when eaten plain or with a light dusting of confectioners' sugar. The batter is even better—my daughters insist I leave them some whenever I make this cake. I warn them about uncooked eggs and salmonella, but I lose all credibility as soon as I get caught licking the spoon. Oh well. Do as I say, not as I do!*

SERVES 8 TO 10

¾ pound (3 sticks) salted
    butter, softened

2 cups sugar

4 large eggs

1 tablespoon vanilla extract

1 cup whole milk

3 cups self-rising flour, sifted

¼ cup confectioners' sugar,
    for dusting

Preheat the oven to 350°F. Grease and flour two round 9-inch cake pans, a loaf pan, or a 13 x 9-inch baking pan.

In a large mixing bowl, beat together the butter and sugar with an electric mixer on medium-high speed until creamy. Add the eggs, one at a time, beating well after each addition.

Combine the vanilla and milk in a bowl, then add the mixture gradually to the butter mixture. Add the flour ½ cup at a time and continue beating until it is fully incorporated. Do not over-beat.

Pour the batter into the prepared pan(s) and bake for 35 to 45 minutes, until a toothpick inserted in the center of the cake comes out clean. Set aside to cool completely.

Just before serving, dust the cake with confectioners' sugar.

Arroz con Leche

RICE PUDDING

Many Cubans adore this decadent, creamy, concoction made with condensed milk. But to be honest, I didn't want to include it in this cookbook. I did it to please my mother, who insisted it be included. (Why I cannot say "no" to that woman, I'll never know.) But Mom says Arroz con Leche *is a very traditional Cuban dessert, and you all will expect it to be in the book. Therefore, in an effort to avoid disappointing all you sweet rice-eating people, here it is.*

Actually, now that I look at the recipe . . . maybe I'll try it after all.

SERVES 8

¾ cup short-grain white rice (Valencia or Italian Arborio rice)

1 tablespoon butter

Half a lime

2 cups whole milk

1 can sweetened condensed milk

½ cup sugar

1 cinnamon stick

¼ teaspoon salt

Ground cinnamon

Bring 2 cups of water to boil in a heavy saucepan over medium-high heat. Add the rice and butter and cook, uncovered, for 5 minutes. Reduce the heat to low, cover the pan, and continue cooking for another 15 minutes. Remove from the heat and set aside.

Using a vegetable peeler, carefully peel away the lime zest, green part only, from the lime. You will be removing this from the pudding later on, so make sure you leave this in larger peelings.

In a large bowl, combine the lime zest, milk, condensed milk, sugar, cinnamon stick, and salt.

Use a fork to fluff up the rice, making sure it is not stuck to the bottom of the pot. Add the milk mixture and return the pan to the stove. Cook over low heat, stirring frequently, for 40 to 50 minutes, until the pudding thickens. Set aside to cool to room temperature, then refrigerate for at least 1 hour, until the pudding sets.

To serve, remove the cinnamon stick and lime zest and sprinkle with a generous amount of cinnamon.

Cheesecake de Guayaba

GUAVA CHEESECAKE

You and I both know that no one ever made cheesecake in Cuba. It is by no means an authentic and traditional Cuban dessert, but this recipe is so good, I had to include it (without consulting my mother, of course). If it is any consolation, guava cheesecake is served at many Cuban restaurants in Miami. But this recipe creates something completely unlike the crumbly, dry cheesecake topped with a thin layer of guava purée that is served at many of these establishments. This one is rich, creamy, and pink, through and through. Yes, pink! The guava marmalade is actually incorporated into the cheese batter, truly making it a guava cheesecake.

You can find guava marmalade, usually in a can, at most supermarkets in the Hispanic food section. For the absolute best results, it really is preferable to use marmalade, but if you can't find it, you can use guava jam or jelly, although the flavor won't be nearly as intense and the cheesecake will be more tan than pink. In a pinch, I've even cubed guava paste and heated it over very low heat, with a little water, to make marmalade. And I don't need to remind you to NOT use fat-free cream cheese, do I?

SERVES 8 TO 10

4 tablespoons salted butter, at room temperature

1½ cups graham cracker crumbs

¾ cup sugar

24 ounces cream cheese (I prefer Philadelphia brand)

1 tablespoon vanilla extract

1½ cup half-and-half

2 cups guava marmalade

Preheat the oven to 400°F.

Combine the butter, graham cracker crumbs, and ¼ cup of the sugar in a bowl. Firmly press this mixture into the bottom and about 1 inch up the sides of an 8- or 9-inch springform pan. Place the pan on a baking sheet and bake for 10 minutes. Set aside to cool. Leave the oven set to 400°F.

In a large bowl, beat the cream cheese, vanilla, and remaining ½ cup sugar with an electric mixer until fluffy. Gradually add the half-and-half and mix until the mixture is thin and free of lumps. Beat in 1 cup of the guava marmalade. Pour the mixture into the cooled pie crust and bake for 15 minutes. Reduce the heat to 300°F and bake for 1 hour and 15 minutes more. Turn off the heat and allow the cheesecake to cool in the oven with the oven door partially open.

Once the cheesecake has reached room temperature, cover it with plastic wrap and refrigerate for at least 6 hours, preferably overnight.

Spread the remaining cup of guava marmalade over the top of the cheesecake before serving.

Tocino del Cielo
EGG YOLK CUSTARD

Here we go again with the funny named recipes. Tocino del Cielo, *literally translated, means "Bacon of the Sky." Some people say it means "Heavenly Bacon." No, there is no bacon in this deliciously sweet egg custard that is coated with caramel. Imagine a super duper concentrated flan. That's my scientific culinary description of* Tocino del Cielo. *Hey, it's better than Bacon of the Sky! Who was in charge of naming desserts in Cuba anyway?*

SERVES 6

2½ cups sugar
1 teaspoon vanilla
12 egg yolks

Combine the sugar, vanilla, and 1½ cups water in a large saucepan and bring to a boil. Cook, stirring frequently, for 12 to 15 minutes, or until the mixture reduces by about one-third. Pour all but ⅓ cup of the syrup into a heatproof bowl and set aside to cool.

Cook the remaining caramel over low heat until it turns light brown. Pour this caramel into six 4- to 6-ounce ramekins.

Preheat the oven to 350°F.

Beat the egg yolks with an electric mixer, then add the cooled syrup little by little, and mix until it is fully incorporated. Strain the mixture through a fine sieve and divide it equally among the ramekins.

Fill a large rectangular baking pan halfway with water. Carefully place the ramekins into the water in the pan, and place the pan on the center rack of the oven. Bake for about 45 minutes, until the centers of the custards are set.

Take the ramekins out of the water and let them cool to room temperature. Refrigerate for at least 4 hours, or up to overnight.

Before serving, run a knife around the sides of the ramekins to loosen the custard. You can also dip the bottom halves of the ramekins in warm (not hot) water for about 30 seconds to ensure the bottom of the custard releases with ease. Invert the cups onto small plates.

Flan de Queso

CREAM CHEESE FLAN

This is a cross between a Cuban flan and a traditional cheesecake. It's a wonderful mix, making a denser, richer flan. This is a great recipe for flan virgins—what I call people who've never made flan. The cream cheese ensures against the little air bubbles that sometimes form when inexperienced people make flan. Basically, it's foolproof flan. Finally, a flan even my brother can make!

SERVES 6

1 cup sugar

4 large eggs

2 large egg yolks

1 (14-ounce) can condensed milk

1 (14-ounce) can evaporated milk

1 teaspoon vanilla extract

8 ounces full-fat cream cheese (none of that low-fat stuff), at room temperature

¼ teaspoon salt

Preheat the oven to 325°F.

Heat ½ cup of the sugar in a small saucepan over medium-low heat, stirring occasionally, for 15 to 20 minutes, until the sugar melts. Watch it closely so that it does not burn. Once the sugar has completely melted and turned a light caramel color, pour it evenly into six 4- to 6-ounce ramekins.

Combine the remaining sugar, the eggs, egg yolks, condensed milk, evaporated milk, vanilla, cream cheese, and salt in a blender, and blend until completely combined. Pour evenly into the ramekins.

Fill a large rectangular baking pan halfway with water. Carefully place the ramekins into the water in the pan, and place the pan on the center rack of the oven. Bake for 40 to 50 minutes, until the centers of the custards are set.

Take the ramekins out of the water and let them cool to room temperature. Refrigerate for 4 hours or overnight.

Before serving, run a knife around the sides of the ramekins to loosen the flan. You can also dip the bottom halves of the ramekins in warm (not hot) water for about 30 seconds to ensure the bottom of the flan releases with ease. Invert the cups onto small plates.

Flan de Coco

COCONUT FLAN

Flan is probably the most common of all Cuban desserts. There are many varieties of flan, this coconut-fla-vored version is a favorite. I like to make my flan in little custard ramekins, and I bake them in a pan filled halfway with water. Cubans call this a baño de Maria, *which is derived from the French term* bain a Marie. *The term makes little sense in any language since it literally translates to Mary's Bath or Mary takes a Bath, neither of which has anything to do with flan. . . . Still, the result is heavenly.*

SERVES 6

¾ cup sugar

4 large eggs

2 large egg yolks

1 (14-ounce) can condensed milk

1 (14-ounce) can evaporated milk

1 teaspoon vanilla extract

¼ teaspoon salt

1 can shredded coconut in heavy syrup, drained, with half of the syrup reserved

Preheat the oven to 325°F.

Heat ½ cup of the sugar in a small saucepan over medium-low heat, stirring occasionally, for 5 to 7 minutes, until the sugar melts. Watch it closely so that it does not burn. Once the sugar has completely melted and turned a light caramel color, pour it evenly into six 4- to 6-ounce ramekins.

Combine the remaining sugar, the eggs, egg yolks, condensed milk, evaporated milk, vanilla, and salt in a blender, and blend until completely combined. Stir in half of the coconut, then pour the mixture into the ramekins. Because the coconut is heavier than the rest of the ingredients, it tends to sit at the bottom of the blender. Use a spoon to divide the coconut evenly among the ramekins, if necessary.

Fill a large rectangular baking pan halfway with water. Carefully set the ramekins in the water, and place the pan on the center rack of the oven. Bake for 40 to 50 minutes, until the centers of the custards are set.

Remove the ramekins from the water-filled pan, and let them cool to room temperature. Refrigerate for at least 4 hours, up to overnight.

Before serving, run a knife around the sides of the ramekins to loosen the flan. You can also dip the bottom halves of the ramekins in some warm (not hot) water for about 30 seconds to ensure the bottom of the flan releases with ease. Invert the cups onto small plates.

Combine the remaining coconut with the reserved syrup.

To serve, place a dollop of the coconut mixture next to each flan.

Pudín de Pan

CUBAN-STYLE BREAD PUDDING

Cuban bread pudding is a little different from the bread pudding that is so in vogue these days. Ours is served chilled and topped with simple syrup instead of a richer crème anglaise *or butter rum sauce. Still, I have also included the recipe for an orange-butter rum sauce that I just adore. I think it goes best with a warm bread pudding. This recipe is delicious either way. You can serve it directly from the fridge or the oven. You can even nuke it for a few seconds. Variety is the spice of life, right?*

SERVES 8

½ cup evaporated milk

1 cup whole milk

1 (14-ounce) can sweetened condensed milk

1 (14-ounce) can lite fruit cocktail, undrained (perhaps the only time you see the word "lite" in this book)

1 teaspoon vanilla extract

½ teaspoon ground cinnamon

½ cup light brown sugar

½ cup sliced almonds, lightly toasted

½ cup raisins

3 tablespoons brandy or amaretto

4 large eggs, beaten

Pinch salt

1 (2-foot) loaf day-old Cuban bread or French bread, torn into 2-inch pieces

6 tablespoons salted butter, melted

Combine the milks, fruit cocktail, vanilla, cinnamon, brown sugar, almonds, raisins, brandy, eggs, and salt in a large bowl and mix until fully incorporated.

In another large bowl, toss the bread with 4 tablespoons of the melted butter.

Use the remaining 2 tablespoons of melted butter to grease a 2-quart Pyrex or glass baking dish.

Pour the milk mixture over the bread and toss well. Allow this mixture to sit for 35 to 45 minutes, until some of the liquid is absorbed by the bread.

Preheat the oven to 350°F.

Pour the bread mixture into the prepared baking pan and bake for 1 to 1½ hours, until the pudding sets.

Serve warm or set aside to cool to room temperature, then refrigerate for 4 hours, or overnight. Top with one of the sauces from the next page.

SIMPLE SYRUP

1 cup sugar

1 cup water

Zest from half a lime

1 stick cinnamon

Pinch salt

Combine all of the ingredients in a small saucepan, and bring the mixture to a boil. Reduce the heat to low and cook until the mixture reduces by half, about 15 to 20 minutes. Remove the cinnamon and lime zest and chill before serving.

ORANGE BUTTER
RUM SAUCE

¼ pound (1 stick) salted butter

¼ cup vanilla-flavored rum
(Bacardi makes a good one)

½ cup orange juice

2 cups confectioners' sugar

¼ cup heavy cream

Melt the butter in a medium saucepan over low heat. Add the rum and orange juice and bring to a boil. Allow the mixture to boil, stirring frequently, for 3 to 5 minutes, in order for alcohol to evaporate. Watch it closely so it doesn't burn. Remove the sauce from the heat, add the sugar, and whisk or beat it with an electric mixer on low until no lumps remain. Add the cream in a steady stream, mixing all the while until fully incorporated. Return the sauce to the stove and simmer over low heat for 5 minutes. Serve warm.

Torrejas
CUBAN-STYLE FRENCH TOAST

Although "Cuban-style French toast" is the best translation of "Torrejas" I could come up with, this treat is traditionally eaten as a dessert and not a breakfast dish. And it's usually served chilled. But what the heck, have it for breakfast, or warm, if you want. What's with all these rules, anyway?

SERVES 8

1 cup canola oil

1 cup whole milk

1 cup evaporated milk

2 teaspoons vanilla extract

3 large egg yolks, beaten

¼ cup *vino seco* (dry white cooking wine)

1 cup sugar

1 teaspoon ground cinnamon

3 large eggs

1 (1-pound) loaf egg or challah bread, cut into 1- to 1½-inch slices

Simple Syrup (page 202), for serving

In a large frying pan, heat the oil over medium heat.

Combine the milk, evaporated milk, vanilla, egg yolks, *vino seco*, sugar, and cinnamon in a large, shallow dish. Place the eggs in another shallow dish and beat them lightly.

Working in batches, dip the bread in the milk mixture, then into the eggs. Carefully place 2 to 3 slices of bread in the hot oil and fry for 2 to 3 minutes on each side, until golden brown. Drain on a paper towel and repeat with the remaining bread. Refrigerate, covered, for 1 hour or serve warm.

Serve with Simple Syrup.

My Big Fat Cuban Torrejas

I have a confession to make. I met someone online. I know, you're probably thinking, 'How dangerous!' I mean, anyone who has ever watched Dateline would avoid meeting strangers on the internet like the plague! But this is different. I met Marta Darby because of her very funny blog, My Big Fat Cuban Family. She posts some of her recipes there, and this version of torrejas stuffed with guava and cream cheese really caught my eye. This delicious creation, which is similar to French toast, is proof that sometimes venturing into cyberspace can lead to some very tasty discoveries and good friendships.

SERVES 4

½ cup to 1 cup vegetable oil

4 egg yolks

1 cup whole milk

2 tablespoons sugar

1 teaspoon cinnamon

1 teaspoon vanilla extract

3 eggs

8 slices thick white bread
(I found something called Texas Toast—extra thick bread—but Cuban bread or French bread work well, too)

12 ounces cream cheese

12 ounces guava paste,
cut into slices

Confectioners' sugar

In a large frying pan, heat just enough oil to cover the pan's surface.

Combine the egg yolks, milk, sugar, cinnamon, and vanilla in a large bowl. Whisk thoroughly and set aside.

In a separate bowl, whisk the eggs.

Spread each slice of bread generously with cream cheese. Place about 4 or 5 thin slices of guava paste on each of the 4 slices of bread and top with the remaining slices to make sandwiches.

Preheat the oven to 400°F.

Create an assembly line of sandwiches, milk mixture, and beaten eggs. Quickly dip the sandwiches into the milk mixture, then into the eggs. Fry them in the hot oil for 2 to 3 minutes per side, just until brown.

Place the sandwiches on a baking dish and bake for about 10 minutes, until the guava melts.

To serve, cut each sandwich into quarters and dust with confectioners' sugar.

Torticas de Moron

CUBAN-STYLE SUGAR COOKIES

When I need a quick sugar fix and my cupboards are barren, this is my recipe of choice. Torticas de Moron *are a classic Cuban treat. They vary from traditional sugar cookies because they are made with shortening instead of butter, giving them a light, crumbly texture. They just melt in your mouth. You can keep these cookies in an airtight container for up to 1 week.*

MAKES ABOUT 3 DOZEN COOKIES

1 cup vegetable shortening (like Crisco)

1 cup sugar, plus more as garnish

3 cups all-purpose flour

½ teaspoon salt

1 teaspoon grated lemon zest

Combine the shortening and sugar in a large bowl and mix well with a wooden spoon. Add the flour, ½ cup at a time, mixing well to incorporate it completely. Stir in the lemon zest.

Turn the dough out onto a piece of plastic wrap and form it into a 2½-inch-wide cylinder. Wrap the plastic around the dough and refrigerate it for at least 1 hour, until the dough becomes slightly firm.

Preheat the oven to 350°F.

Cut the dough into ½-inch slices and place them on a parchment paper–lined baking sheet. Bake for 20 to 25 minutes, until golden brown.

After taking the cookies out of the oven, immediately sprinkle them with additional sugar.

Merenguitos
MERINGUE COOKIES

I confess, this recipe is not my own. It was created by Yolanda, the mother of my friend, Juan Alonso. I had to give you Yolanda's recipe because, for some reason, whenever I use any other method to make this seemingly simple recipe of egg whites and sugar, it never works out. My cookies end up kind of hollow and chewy. Yolanda's recipe, however, is perfection, resulting in cookies that are crispy and toasty. So now you know it: I'm not perfect. It just seems that way. It's an illusion.

For fancier merenguitos, *pipe them onto parchment paper using a star-tipped cake decorating bag.*

MAKES 24 COOKIES

3 large egg whites
⅛ teaspoon cream of tartar
1 cup sugar

Preheat the oven to 300°F. Line 2 baking sheets with parchment paper.

Combine the egg whites and cream of tartar in a medium-sized bowl and beat them with an electric mixer on medium speed until soft peaks form. Gradually add the sugar, then beat on high speed until the whites are stiff and shiny.

Drop the egg whites by rounded tablespoonfuls onto the prepared baking sheets, spaced 1 inch apart. Bake for 25 minutes, until the cookies are dry. Turn the oven off and allow the *merenguitos* to rest in the oven for at least 12 hours or overnight.

BEBIDAS
BEVERAGES

Cubans are not particularly fond of water as a beverage unless, of course, they are taking a pill prescribed by their cousin who was a doctor in Cuba. Generally, we do not favor it as an accompaniment to food. Wine is good, but unlike the Spaniards or French, it is not at our everyday dinner tables. Cubans do enjoy an occasional *fría* (literal translation: cold; Cuban slang: beer) now and again, but soft drinks and fruit shakes are pretty much our preference.

Soft drinks, like Coke and Pepsi, are popular, but many Cubans consume other less common soft drinks. Three in particular come to mind: *Jupiña, Materva,* and *Ironbeer.* These soft drinks are sweet and uniquely flavored. Sweet is important. After all, Cubans enjoy pure sugar cane juice called *Guarapo* regularly, which ironically is said to keep us regular. *Jupiña* is a pineapple-flavored soft drink. The name says it all "Ju" is short for *jugo* (juice), and "piña" means pineapple. Funny thing is that while it is delicious, this beverage probably has very little pineapple juice in it. *Materva,* I suppose, is flavored with *yerba mate,* a potent herb that contains lots of caffeine (very popular in South America). *Ironbeer* was always my little brother's favorite. You see, he was a 90-pound weakling with a bodybuilder father and a sister who constantly taunted him. The can featured an impressive picture of a strong man flexing his rather large bicep. Naturally, my brother was certain that drinking this beverage in mass quantities would make him strong like, say, . . . iron? Instead, he was consuming so much caffeine, it had him bouncing off the walls (making him even more adorable).

I would hate to mislead anyone into believing that Cubans do not enjoy alcoholic beverages. Perish the thought! We love beer, mojitos, and *Cuba Líbres* (which literally translates as free Cuba). Give a Cuban a couple of mojitos, and he or she will be dancing to the beat of his or her own bongos. I think you will really enjoy all the drinks featured in this chapter, from the traditional *Café con Leche* to the party time *Whammy.* Why not give them all a try?

Chocolate Caliente
HOT CHOCOLATE

It is common knowledge that it does not get very cold in Miami. On the rare occasion when the temperature dips way down into the sixties, Cubans go out and get three things: a sweater, hot chocolate, and churros (deep-fried dough sticks sprinkled with sugar). I am sure you already own a sweater, and really good churros are complicated and require special equipment. However, no "cold" day in Miami is complete without a mug of wickedly rich and sweet Cuban-style hot chocolate. But whatever you do, please, please do not add marshmallows to this! It would be sacrilege.

In this recipe, I call for Menier sweet chocolate, which you can find in the baking section of your grocery store or where the powdered hot chocolate mixes are found. But if you can't find it, any sweet baking chocolate will do.

SERVES 6

½ cup evaporated milk

½ cup sweetened
  condensed milk

1 (8-ounce) bar Menier sweet
  chocolate, finely chopped

3 cups whole milk

Pinch of salt

Sugar

Combine the evaporated and condensed milks in a large saucepan and bring to a boil. Immediately reduce the heat to medium-low, then add the chocolate, stirring until it melts. Whisk in the whole milk 1 cup at a time. Add the salt. Cover the pan, reduce the heat to low, and simmer for 30 minutes. Add sugar to taste.

Café con Leche

CUBAN COFFEE WITH MILK

Café con leche *is one of those things that most Cubans cannot live without. It is as essential to us as anyone else's morning cup of joe and is definitely as addictive. The difference is that Cubans give* café con leche *to their kids as well. I wonder how many ADD diagnoses would have been prevented by eliminating this practice altogether. . . . Well, too late for me.*

Serve this steaming hot with Cuban toast and butter. Oh, and don't forget to dip the bread in it! Oh, don't pretend you've never done it.

SERVES 1

4 ounces whole milk

2 ounces evaporated milk

1 to 2 ounces prepared Cuban
  coffee or espresso

2 tablespoons sugar,
  or less depending on taste
  (I like it sweet)

Small pinch salt

Combine the whole milk and the evaporated milk in a small saucepan and bring to a boil. Pour into a large mug and add the coffee and sugar, to taste. Add the tiniest pinch of salt.

Cortadito
CUBAN COFFEE WITH A SHOT OF MILK

The cortadito *has always been a Cuban favorite, and has become so popular in recent years that you can order it at almost any Miami restaurant. A* cortadito *is a combination of Cuban espresso—cafecito—and a small amount of steamed milk. The milk is usually whole milk, evaporated milk, or a combination of the two, which I believe tastes best. Please do not attempt to make this with low fat or (perish the thought) skim milk. It simply does not work. The end result is grayish and thin and not at all worthy of the name* cortadito. *Enjoy a steaming hot cup after a large meal as you sit back, pants let out (or completely unbuttoned), and doze off to the sound of your favorite* novela *(Latino soap opera).*

SERVES 4 TO 6

3 ounces evaporated milk

3 ounces whole milk

6 ounces freshly prepared
  Cuban coffee or espresso

Sugar

Combine the evaporated and whole milks in a small saucepan and bring to a boil (you can do this in the microwave, but I promise you it will not taste the way it should). Watch it closely, as it can easily boil over. Let stand a minute or two until a film forms on top of the milk. Remove the film and pour the milk into 6 small cups and top with coffee to desired darkness. Add sugar to taste.

Batido de Platano

BANANA SHAKE

My particular technique for making banana shakes came about when I bought too many bananas one day. Instead of throwing away the ones that were too ripe to eat, I peeled them, wrapped them in plastic, and froze them in a large freezer bag. Frozen ripe bananas are so sweet, they require little to no sugar or ice in a milkshake. And they make the best banana shakes this side of Havana.

SERVES 1

1 frozen banana, cut into small chunks

2 tablespoons condensed milk

1 cup cold whole milk

¼ cup cold evaporated milk

1 tablespoon sugar, or more to taste

1 teaspoon vanilla extract

Combine all of the ingredients in a blender and blend until smooth and creamy. Pour into a tall glass and enjoy!

Batido de Mamey

MAMEY MILKSHAKE

Mamey is a tropical fruit native to Mexico and Central America but it is also found in Cuba and Puerto Rico. It is football shaped with a rough skin and a red-orange dense interior. The fruit's single large seed is said to be poisonous if ingested. (So don't ingest the seed, ok?) The fruit is only available for a few months of the year, which is why its pulp is often sold frozen. You can find it online or in the Hispanic frozen food section of most large supermarkets.

There are two schools of thought when it comes to preparing mamey milkshakes: using frozen mamey pulp or mamey ice cream as a base for the shake. I provide you with directions for making both below. While both are delicious, I prefer to use frozen mamey pulp. You can also make the milkshake with fresh mamey by adding some ice and sugar to the recipe below.

SERVES 1

Using mamey pulp

8 ounces whole milk
  (you know how I feel
  about skim milk)

4 ounces frozen mamey pulp

4 tablespoons sweetened
  condensed milk

Sugar, to taste

Using mamey ice cream

6 ounces whole milk

2 large scoops mamey
  ice cream

Sugar, to taste

Combine all ingredients in a blender and blend until smooth and creamy. Serve immediately.

Batido de Trigo
WHEAT MILK SHAKE

Batido de Trigo *is uniquely Cuban. It is quite delicious and is made using puffed wheat cereal. Yup, you read that correctly, puffed wheat—doesn't that sound healthy? Well, it is! Another healthy recipe brought to you by ¡Sabor!*

SERVES 1

1 cup puffed wheat cereal

1 cup cold whole milk

2 tablespoons malted
    milk powder

2 tablespoons condensed milk

1 tablespoon sugar,
    or more to suit your taste

2 or 3 ice cubes

Combine all of the ingredients in a blender and blend until creamy. Pour into a tall glass and enjoy!

Cuba Libre
RUM AND COKE

This drink became popular after the first Cuban immigrants arrived to the United States. The drink, aptly named Cuba Libre, *literally translates to Free Cuba. I guess you could call this a dream in a glass. Unfortunately, Cuba has never since been free (. . . yet). Perhaps a few of these will make it easier to remember a time when it was, or imagine a time when it will be again.*

SERVES 1

Ice cubes or crushed ice

1 wedge lime

1 ounce white rum
  (like Bacardi)

3 ounces Coca Cola

Fill a tumbler or old-fashioned glass with ice and squeeze the wedge of lime into it. Pour in the rum and top with the cola. Give it a stir and enjoy.

Piña Colada

Did you know that the Piña Colada was Puerto Rico's national drink? Neither did I. I guess I should feel a little guilty including it in my Cuban cookbook, no? No! After all, Cubans and Puerto Ricans are so similar— we share the same language, have similar cultures, even our flags are similar! Plus, the Piña Colada has so many tropical elements, I just had to include it. I am sure our Puerto Rican friends won't mind!

SERVES 1

4 ounces pineapple juice

2 ounces coconut cream (Coco
  Lopez makes a good one)

2 ounces light rum

¼ cup crushed ice

½ slice pineapple, for garnish

1 maraschino cherry, for garnish

Combine the pineapple juice, coconut cream, and rum in a blender add blend for 30 seconds. Add the ice and blend a few seconds more. Pour into a tall glass or goblet and garnish with the pineapple slice and cherry. Serve immediately.

Daiquirí

The original daiquirí—made of rum, lime, and sugar—was created in Cuba in 1896 by an American mining engineer named Jennings Cox. He named the drink after the Cuban town of Daiquirí. Some say he ran out of gin and had to "make do" with rum. Hemingway was famous for drinking this classic concoction at El Floridita restaurant in Havana. It is said he often lingered at the bar for hours on end ordering doubles—later named Papa Dobles—which contained 4 full ounces of rum.

SERVES 1

2 ounces light Bacardi rum

2 teaspoons superfine sugar

1 ounce fresh lime juice

1 tablespoon triple sec, optional

½ cup crushed ice

1 slice lime, for garnish

Combine the rum, sugar, lime juice, triple sec, and ice in a blender and blend for 20 to 30 seconds. Pour into a chilled glass and garnish with the lime slice. Serve immediately.

Mojito

A mojito, as many of you know, is a lime and mint flavored drink that has become very popular. The wonderful thing about the mojito is that it is lightly tart and refreshing like a lemonade with just enough sweetness to keep you from noticing the massive amount of rum! In my opinion, the bartender at the Miami restaurant Ortanique, Joel, makes the best mojitos . . . dare I say it? . . . in the world!

Recently, my friend Percy taught me the distinction between mojitos and mojitos criollos. Turns out, mojitos criollos are prepared without Angostura bitters. This recipe is for the traditional mojito, with bitters. Since mojitos have become so popular, now you can find muddlers—the tool used to crush the mint—at most kitchen stores.

SERVES 1

6 fresh mint leaves, plus
    more for garnish

2 teaspoons sugar

Juice from 1 lime, about
    3 tablespoons

1 ounce white rum
    (like Bacardi)

2 tablespoons triple sec

Splash sparkling or soda water

2 or 3 drops Angostura bitters

Lime slices, for garnish

Combine the mint and sugar in a cocktail shaker. Use a muddler to crush the leaves together with the sugar. Add the lime juice, rum, and triple sec, and shake well. Pour into a tall glass filled with ice. Add the sparkling water over it and top with a few drops of bitters. Garnish with slices of lime and mint.

Whammy

I will confess that I did not obtain this recipe in an honorable fashion. Because its creator was not inclined to share the recipe with anyone, I bribed his son-in-law into giving me his version of the drink based exclusively on the evidence obtained by rummaging through the creator's garbage (I kid you not). I am still not certain if the recipe is 100% accurate, but after testing it, and testing it, and testing it—did I say I tested it?—it is pretty close. I suppose this is similar to a rum punch or a Mai Tai, but it has a unique flavor all its own. You really must try it.

SERVES 1

4 ounces orange juice (no pulp)

½ ounce key lime juice
   (freshly squeezed)

1 tablespoon grenadine syrup

1 ounce Nassau Royale Rum

1 teaspoon sugar

1 ounce Bacardi white rum

Combine all of the ingredients in a shaker and mix well. Pour over ice and enjoy.

Sangria

While sangria originated in Spain, it is quite popular among Cubans, almost certainly due to its sweetness. Be warned, the combination of ingredients is potent and will get you when you least expect it. You've been warned. Now drink up.

SERVES 12

½ cup brandy
  (preferably Spanish)
1 cup lemonade
Juice of 1 orange, about ¼ cup
2 tablespoons superfine sugar,
  or more to taste
1 (750 ml) bottle red table wine
½ cup soda water
1 orange, sliced
1 lemon, sliced
1 red apple, cored and cubed
Ice cubes

Combine the brandy, lemonade, orange juice, and sugar in a large pitcher and mix well. Add the wine, soda water, and fruit, and stir. Fill the pitcher halfway with ice cubes and serve immediately.

White Sangria

A little lighter and less sweet than its red counterpart, white sangria is a wonderful accompaniment to less hearty dishes like Arroz con Camarones *(page 175) and* Pescado en Salsa Verde *(page 180). Less hearty . . . who am I kidding?*

SERVES 12

½ cup triple sec

1 cup lemonade

Juice of 1 lemon, about
   3 tablespoons

2 tablespoons superfine sugar,
   or more to taste

1 (750 ml) bottle white
   table wine

½ cup soda water

1 orange, sliced

1 lemon, sliced

1 green apple, cored and cubed

Ice cubes

Combine the triple sec, lemonade, lemon juice, and sugar in a large pitcher and mix well. Add the wine, soda water, and fruit, and stir. Fill the pitcher halfway with ice cubes and serve immediately.

❋ SAMPLE MENUS ❋

SAMPLE MENU 1

Ensalada de Aguacate (Avocado Salad)
  (page 121)
Arroz con Pollo (Chicken with Rice) (page 158)
Tostones (Fried Green Plantains) (page 97)
Flan de Coco (Coconut Flan) (page 198)
Cortadito (Cuban Coffee with Milk) (page 213)

SAMPLE MENU 2

Croqueta Preparada (Croquette Sandwich)
  (page 64)
Mariquitas (Fried Plantain Chips) with *Mojo
  Criollo* (Garlic Sauce) (pages 99 and 93)
Batido de Mamey (Mamey Milkshake)
  (page 216)

SAMPLE MENU 3

Ensalada Cubana (Cuban-Style Green Salad)
  (page 117)
Camarones Enchilados (Shrimp Creole)
  (page 176)
Arroz Blanco (White Rice) (page 82)
Platanitos Maduros (Fried Sweet Plantains)
  (page 94)
Natilla (Vanilla Custard) (page 190)

SAMPLE MENU 4

Ensalada de Tomate y Cebolla
  (Tomato and Onion Salad) (page 116)
Pollo Asado (Roast Chicken) (page 161)
Moros (Black Beans and Rice) (page 88)
Tostones (Fried Green Plantains) (page 97)
Pudin de Pan (Cuban-Style Bread Pudding)
  (page 201)

SAMPLE MENU 5

Chicharos (Split Pea Soup) (page 51)
Vaca Frita (Stir-Fried Beef) (page 141)
Arroz Blanco (White Rice) (page 82)
Papitas Fritas (French Fried Potatoes)
  (page 91)
Flan de Coco (Coconut Flan) (page 198)

SAMPLE MENU 6

Frijoles Negros (Black Bean Soup) (page 40)
Arroz Blanco (White Rice) (page 82)
Bistec de Palomilla (Minute Steak) (page 138)
Platanitos Maduros (Fried Ripe Plantains)
  (page 94)
Tita's Panetela (My Mom's Famous
  Butter Pound Cake) (page 191)

SAMPLE MENU 7
Ajiaco (Meat and Vegetable Stew) (pages 48-49)
Arroz Blanco (White Rice) (page 82)
Pan de Ajo (Cuban Garlic Bread) (page 79)
Arroz con Leche (Rice Pudding) (page 193)

SAMPLE MENU 8
COCKTAIL PARTY MENU
Empanadas de Carne (Beef Turnovers)
   (page 24)
Croquetas de Jamón (Ham Croquettes)
   (pages 26-28)
Frituras de Bacalao (Cod Fritters) (page 29)
Queso Brie Envuelto con Guayaba
   (Brie and Guava en Croûte) (page 21)
Ensalada de Pollo (Chicken Salad) (page 120)
Mini Fritas Cubana (Mini Cuban Hamburgers)
   (page 73)
Cuba Libre (Rum and Coke) (page 218)
Whammy (page 222)
Mojito (page 221)

SAMPLE MENU 9
THANKSGIVING DAY MENU
Empanadas de Chorizo (Chorizo Turnovers)
   (page 23)
Pavo de Thanksgiving con Relleno de Jamón
   (Thanksgiving Day Turkey with Ham Stuffing)
   (page 169)
Moros o Congri (Black or Red Beans and Rice)
   (pages 88 and 87)
Yuca con Mojo Criollo (Yuca with Garlic Sauce)
   (page 93)
Mariquitas (Fried Plantain Chips) (page 99)
Cheesecake de Guayaba (Guava Cheesecake)
   (page 194)

SAMPLE MENU 10
CHRISTMAS EVE MENU
Croquetas de Pollo (Chicken Croquettes)
   (pages 26-28)
Ensalada de Aguacate (Avocado Salad)
   (page 121)
Pierna Asada (Roast Pork Leg) (page 132)
Yuca con Mojo Criollo (Yuca with Garlic Sauce)
   (page 93)
Congri (Red Beans and Rice) (page 87)
Torrejas (Cuban-Style French Toast) (page 203)

✳ GLOSSARY ✳

Ajiaco: A hearty meat and vegetable stew.

Annatto: A red food coloring and flavoring used in many Latin American cuisines. It comes from the seeds of achiote trees and is a major ingredient in the Sazón spice blends by Goya Foods and in Bijol.

Bijol: See *annatto*.

Boniato: A type of sweet potato, commonly called Cuban Sweet Potato.

Café con leche: Translated as "coffee with milk." A glass of Cuban coffee, or espresso, served alongside a cup of steamed milk. The coffee is then poured into the milk and drunk.

Calabaza: Commonly called a Cuban Squash, the *calabaza* is a hybrid between a pumpkin and a squash. It has green or yellow skin and yellow-orange flesh.

Chicharos: Split peas.

Chorizo: Spanish pork sausage, with a distinct red coloring that comes from paprika.

Congri: Red beans with rice.

Croqueta preparada: A Cuban sandwich with two ham croquettes added to the inside.

Cuban bread: Bread, similar to French and Italian bread, made with lard instead of oil. It has a hard, thin, almost papery crust and a soft flaky middle. It is often baked with a long, moist palm frond on top of the loaves, creating a shallow trench in the upper crust.

Cuban coffee: Espresso, to which sugar is added during the brewing process.

Cortadito: Translated as "short one," this is a Cuban coffee topped with steamed milk.

Fabas: Butter beans or lima beans.

Fideos: Very thin noodles, similar to vermicelli or angel hair pasta.

Frijoles colorados: Red beans.

Guava: Guavas are a dense fruit with green skin and white to pink pulp. They can be extremely sweet to tart, depending on their ripeness.

Harina: In Spanish, *harina* means flour. However, this term is also used for the cornmeal mixture that is used to make corn tortillas and tamales, as in *masa harina*.

Jamón serrano: Spanish dry-cured ham, sliced thin, similar to Italian prosciutto.

Lacón: Pork shoulder.

Lechón asado: Whole roasted pig.

Maduros: Fried sweet, or mature, plantains.

Malanga: A root vegetable, similar to the taro and cassava, with a woodsy taste.

Mamey: A tropical fruit with a light pink to a deep salmon pulp and a flavor of sweet pumpkin with a hint of berry.

Mariquitas: Plantain chips.

Mojo: A signature marinade of Cuba, made from garlic and sour orange juice.

Morcilla: Spanish blood pudding.

Moros: Black beans with rice, often called *Moros y Cristianos* (Moors and Christians).

Palomilla: Thinly-cut top sirloin steaks. A common cut of meat in Latin communities.

Picadillo: Cuban-style meat hash.

Pimentón: Smoked paprika, used to flavor Spanish chorizos and paella. Often comes in three varieties—sweet and mild (*dulce*), bittersweet medium hot (*agridulce*), and hot (*picante*).

Sabor: Flavor, taste, spirit.

Sofrito: A fragrant sauce made of garlic, onion, tomato, and bell peppers that forms the base of many Cuban dishes.

Sour orange: Also known as bitter or Seville oranges, these oranges have a very tart juice, and form the basis for many Cuban marinades and sauces.

Tamales: Cornmeal dough filled with a sweet or savory filling, wrapped in corn husks or banana leaves and boiled or steamed.

Tasajo: Salt-cured and dried beef.

Tostones: Green, or unripe, plantains that are cut into slices, fried, flattened, and fried again.

Valencia rice: Valencia rice takes its name from the Valencia province of Spain. Also known as Spanish, paella, or pearl rice, this is a short-grain rice.

Vino Seco: A fortified dry cooking wine that is the one exception to the "not good enough to drink not good enough to cook with rule." It is a must for Cuban recipes, but not the kind of wine you could ever fathom drinking. It tastes like anti-freeze but imparts a delicious and unique flavor to food.

Yuca: Also known as cassava, *yuca* (yucca in English) a starchy root similar in size and texture to the malanga. It has white flesh and a dark brown skin, and texture like a potato.

✳ SOURCES GUIDE ✳

Many, if not all, of the distinctly Cuban ingredients in this book can be found at a Hispanic or Latin market. However, if your neighborhood doesn't have any of these—yet!—the internet provides another great resource. Here are some of the best sources online.

www.amigofoods.com

Based in Miami, this website has many useful ingredients, including Serrano ham.
(800) 627-2544

www.amazon.com

Amazon is a surprisingly wonderful resource for gourmet food, including Cuban coffee and Serrano ham.

www.cubanfoodmarket.com

A very thorough resource for all things Cuban, including El Palacio Tuna.
(877) 999-9945
Fax: (305) 644-6490
Retail store:
3100 SW 8th St
Miami, FL 33135

www.ellatinazo.com

Another Latin supermarket, featuring Cuban and any kind of Latin American and Cuban ingredients and groceries. A great place for Cuban bread and coffee.
(877) 628-8887

www.hotpaella.com

A beautiful website featuring Spanish products, including Fabes de Asturias, chorizo, Spanish olive oil, and saffron.
(888) 377-2622

www.igourmet.com

(877) 446-8763

www.latinmerchant.com

The online store for El Mercado Latino, located in the world famous Pike Place Market in downtown Seattle, Washington. Specializes in Latin foods and Latin food related products.
(206) 223-9374

www.latinpantry.com

A great online store for Latin ingredients. This is a great place to get guava marmalade.

www.melissas.com

This produce distributor has many unusual fruits and vegetables that can easily be bought online, including boniato, calabaza, malanga, and yuca. Its Monthly Exotic Fruit Club is also a great way to explore unusual fruits and vegetables.

www.mexgrocer.com

Online grocery for authentic Mexican food, cooking utensils, Mexican food recipes, cooking tips, cookbooks, and religious goods and jewelry from Mexico. A great place to buy Bijol, fideos, and sazón.
(877) 463-9476

www.tienda.com

Another beautiful site that sells everything Spanish, including pimentón, Serrano ham, bacalao, chorizo, saffron, and more.
(800) 710-4304
Retail store:
3601 La Grange Parkway
Toano, VA 23168

✳ CONVERSION TABLES ✳

Formulas for Metric Conversion

Ounces to grams	multiply ounces by 28.35
Pounds to grams	multiply pounds by 453.5
Cups to liters	multiply cups by .24
Fahrenheit to Centigrade	subtract 32 from Fahrenheit, multiply by five and divide by 9

Metric Equivalents for Volume

U.S.	Metric	
⅛ tsp.	0.6 ml	
½ tsp.	2.5 ml	
¾ tsp.	4.0 ml	
1 tsp.	5.0 ml	
1½ tsp.	7.0 ml	
2 tsp.	10.0 ml	
3 tsp.	15.0 ml	
4 tsp.	20.0 ml	
1 Tbsp.	—	15.0 ml
1½ Tbsp.	—	22.0 ml
2 Tbsp. (⅛ cup)	1 fl. oz	30.0 ml
2½ Tbsp.	—	37.0 ml
3 Tbsp.	—	44.0 ml
⅓ cup	—	57.0 ml
4 Tbsp. (¼ cup)	2 fl. oz	59.0 ml
5 Tbsp.	—	74.0 ml
6 Tbsp.	—	89.0 ml
8 Tbsp. (½ cup)	4 fl. oz	120.0 ml
¾ cup	6 fl. oz	178.0 ml
1 cup	8 fl. oz	237.0 ml (.24 liters)
1½ cups	—	354.0 ml
1¾ cups	—	414.0 ml
2 cups (1 pint)	16 fl. oz	473.0 ml
4 cups (1 quart)	32 fl. oz	(.95 liters)
5 cups	—	(1.183 liters)
16 cups (1 gallon)	128 fl. oz	(3.8 liters)

Oven Temperatures

Degrees Fahrenheit	Degrees Centigrade	British Gas Marks
200°	93°	—
250°	120°	—
275°	140°	1
300°	150°	2
325°	165°	3
350°	175°	4
375°	190°	5
400°	200°	6
450°	230°	8

Metric Equivalents for Weight

U.S.	Metric
1 oz	28 g
2 oz	58 g
3 oz	85 g
4 oz (¼ lb.)	113 g
5 oz	142 g
6 oz	170 g
7 oz	199 g
8 oz (½ lb.)	227 g
10 oz	284 g
12 oz (¾ lb.)	340 g
14 oz	397 g
16 oz (1 lb.)	454 g

Metric Equivalents for Butter

U.S.	Metric
2 tsp.	10.0 g
1 Tbsp.	15.0 g
1½ Tbsp.	22.5 g
2 Tbsp. (1 oz)	55.0 g
3 Tbsp.	70.0 g
¼ lb. (1 stick)	110.0 g
½ lb. (2 sticks)	220.0 g

Metric Equivalents for Length

U.S.	Metric
¼ inch	.65 cm
½ inch	1.25 cm
1 inch	2.50 cm
2 inches	5.00 cm
3 inches	6.00 cm
4 inches	8.00 cm
5 inches	11.00 cm
6 inches	15.00 cm
7 inches	18.00 cm
8 inches	20.00 cm
9 inches	23.00 cm
12 inches	30.50 cm
15 inches	38.00 cm

✳ NOTES ✳